Hands-On Math Around the Year

by Jacqueline Clarke

SCHOLASTIC
PROFESSIONAL BOOKS

New York • Toronto • London • Auckland • Sydney • Mexico City • New Delhi • Hong Kong

For Bob,
whose support made it all possible

For Deborah Schecter,
who believed in me

Thanks to Joan Novelli for her hard work and guidance

"How to Talk to Your Snowman" by Beverly McLoughland. Copyright © 1990 by Beverly
McLoughland. Reprinted by permission of the author who controls all rights.
"Pebbles" by Valerie Worth. From SMALL POEMS by Valerie Worth. Copyright
© 1972 by Valerie Worth. Reprinted by permission of Farrar, Straus & Giroux.
"Rocks" by Florence Parry Heide. Copyright © 1969 by Florence Parry Heide.
Reprinted by permission of the author.

Produced by Joan Novelli
Interior design by Mo Bing Chan
Cover design by Jaime Lucero
Cover art by Susan Swan
Interior art by Shelley Dieterichs

ISBN 0-590-96725-8

Contents

#

About This Book

The idea for *Hands-On Math Around the Year* came as a result of two obstacles I encountered as a teacher. First, I began bringing objects from nature into the classroom to celebrate the change in seasons and make students more aware of what was happening in the world around them. The problem was, I didn't quite know what to do with those objects. I'd pass them around for observation and read a few pieces of related literature, but I knew that I could be doing more. Second, I began to realize that the only way my students were going to reach independence within the area of mathematics was to provide them with continuous practice on the same skills—computation, problem solving, and so on.

My solution? *Hands-On Math Around the Year*. I decided that if I could bring in a different natural object every few weeks and let students use it as a math manipulative to practice skills, not only would they learn more about nature, but they would strengthen mathematical skills without losing interest.

Hands-On Math Around the Year provides mathematical activities using natural objects for each season of the year. These activities support children's learning in many ways, including:

- providing a natural link between math and science
- increasing students' enjoyment of mathematics
- contributing to positive attitudes toward mathematics
- providing repeated practice of mathematical skills and concepts using different materials
- encouraging an appreciation of nature
- incorporating science process skills
- providing mathematical units that can be used as part of a broader study
- making math integration easier for teachers

Tip

The activities in *Hands-On Math Around the Year* are based on skills and concepts that correlate with the standards recommended by the National Council of Teachers of Mathematics. To see how each section supports the standards, check the chart on page 8.

Using This Book

The activities in this book are divided into sections according to the objects from nature that they explore. These sections are organized by the seasons of a traditional school year, starting with fall topics such as corn, leaves, pumpkins, and apples, and wrapping up with a look to summer and gardens, flowers, seashells, and sand. You can select from the activities to meet your needs. For example, the section on twigs (see page 51) is included in a grouping of winter themes, but you can easily use the activities in any season. In some instances, however, you'll need to stick more closely to the season. "A Patch of Pumpkins," for example (see page 25), is included with fall topics. You'll want to plan these activities accordingly, due to limited availability of pumpkins in other seasons.

Here's an overview of what you'll find for each section.

- **Related Themes:** You can incorporate any of the sections in this book into a broader study. Possibilities are listed at the beginning of each section.

- **Hands-On Activities:** Each section features math activities using the seasonal object. Key math skills/concepts are listed, along with materials and step-by-step instructions.

- **Extra, Extra:** These suggestions show how to integrate nature with other areas of the curriculum. Literature connections make it easy to support your math program with children's books.

- **Reproducible Activity Pages:** These ready-to-use student pages provide additional support for your math program.

You'll find record sheets, patterns, games, and more.

Hands-On Math Mystery Bags

Once you've begun to use *Hands-On Math Around the Year* on a regular basis, students will look forward to finding out about the next seasonal object. Take advantage of their curiosity by combining an introduction to the unit with a "Mystery Bag" lesson on properties.

List the seasonal object's properties (color, shape, size, and texture) on a chart. Hide the seasonal object in a bag and share the chart with students. Ask them to figure out what is in the mystery bag by thinking about what they already know about the object's properties. List their answers on chart paper. Reveal the new seasonal object and demonstrate for students the process you went through in determining its properties.

After repeated exposure to this activity, students will be able to identify the properties of an object independently. Provide opportunities for this by placing an object (other than the seasonal object) at a center. Stock the center with various tools for measuring, including rulers, tape measures, string, scales, and so on. List vocabulary words on charts to assist students in describing properties. Have them record information on a record sheet. (See sample, right.) Once all students have visited the cen-

ter, go over the object's properties as a class and have students review their information. Change the object at the center on a regular basis, such as weekly, to provide further practice. Select objects that relate to your curriculum, or have students take turns providing the objects.

Collaborative Big Books

Here are some suggestions for creating Big Books that support your *Hands-On Math Around the Year* lessons.

The Big Book of Seasons: Divide a blank Big Book into four sections—one for each season. As you introduce each seasonal object, draw or photograph it and add it to the book. Take walks outdoors during each season and draw or photograph other signs of the season to add to the Big Book.

Field Guides: In most cases, the seasonal objects used within this book can be broken down into many different types—for example, corn can be sweet corn, popcorn, flint corn, and so on. Involve students in collecting as many variations as possible. Create a field guide for each seasonal object that includes drawings or photographs of each variation along with its name and other pertinent information.

The Big Book of Tongue Twisters: Invite students to create tongue twisters for each seasonal object. For example, *Peter picked pretty pinecones painted with pink paint.* Draw or photograph the object and place it with the tongue twisters in a Big Book.

The Mystery Bag Big Book: Turn the Mystery Bag charts (see page 6) into a Big

Book that will help students compare one week's object with another. The information on the charts will provide a point of reference for students when guessing new seasonal objects. For example, you might tell students that the new seasonal object is twice as long as the pinecone, has the same shape as the apple, and is the same texture as the twigs.

Seasonal Display Table

With the beginning of each new season, decorate a table with colors and natural objects that represent that season. Invite students to collect objects from home to add to the table. As you introduce each new seasonal object, add it to the display. Add seasonal artwork, writing, and projects. At the end of each season, gather students around the display table and ask questions, such as:

- *Have any of the objects changed? How?*
- *How are the objects alike? How are they different?*
- *Which is the longest (shortest, heaviest, lightest) object?*
- *Do any of these objects begin with the letter A? (Continue with other letters.)*
- *Are any of these objects bumpy? (Continue with other textures.)*
- *Are any of these objects red? (Continue with other colors.)*
- *Are any of these objects cone-shaped? (Continue with other shapes.)*
- *Which of these objects can we eat?*

NCTM
Standards Correlations

	Mathematics as Problem Solving	Mathematics as Communication	Mathematics as Reasoning	Mathematical Connections	Estimation	Number Sense and Numeration	Concepts of Whole Number Operations	Whole Number Computation	Geometry and Spatial Sense	Measurement	Statistics and Probability	Fractions and Decimals	Patterns and Relationships
Closeup on Corn	✿	✿	✿	✿	✿	✿	✿		✿	✿	✿	✿	✿
Looking at Leaves	✿	✿	✿	✿						✿	✿		✿
A Patch of Pumpkins	✿	✿	✿	✿	✿	✿	✿	✿	✿		✿	✿	
All About Apples	✿	✿	✿	✿			✿	✿	✿			✿	✿
Exploring Nuts and Cones	✿	✿	✿	✿		✿	✿		✿	✿	✿	✿	✿
Five, Six, Pick Up Sticks	✿	✿	✿	✿	✿				✿	✿	✿		✿
Investigating Snow and Ice	✿	✿	✿	✿	✿	✿			✿	✿	✿	✿	
Finding Out About Feathers	✿	✿	✿	✿			✿	✿	✿		✿	✿	✿
From Seeds to Flowers	✿	✿	✿	✿			✿			✿	✿		
I Spy Shells	✿	✿	✿	✿			✿		✿	✿		✿	✿
Rounding Up Rocks	✿	✿	✿	✿			✿	✿	✿		✿	✿	
Dig Into Sand	✿	✿	✿	✿	✿	✿	✿			✿		✿	

Closeup On Corn

Most students have seen corn—in a field, on the dinner table, or even as part of the setting in a movie. With these activities, they'll take a closer look at this fall harvest crop. They'll sort corn products, estimate and count the number of popcorn kernels in a jar, measure the amount of time it takes for the first kernel to pop, create patterned bracelets with Indian corn, graph data they collect about corn, and more.

- **Related Themes: Fall, Trees, Plants, Fruits**

Harvest Pattern Bracelets

Explore patterns as students create bracelets from different-colored corn kernels.

Skills and Concepts: patterns, counting

Steps

1 Place the ribbon, kernels, and glue at a center.

2 Invite students to visit the center and use the kernels to create repeated color patterns (for example, red, red, yellow; red, red, yellow).

3 Once students find a pattern they like, have them glue the kernels to the ribbon. They should leave approximately one inch open at each end.

4 Help students glue Velcro to each end of their bracelets. Let dry before wearing.

⊚ **Materials** ⊚

- **8-by-1-inch strips of ribbon** (one for each student)
- **Indian corn kernels from three cobs or one bag of colored popcorn**
- **glue**
- **Velcro** (cut into 1-inch pieces)

How Do You Eat Your Corn?

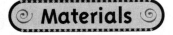

Materials

- **one ear of corn**
- **paper**
- **pencils**
- **graph markers** (see page 16)
- **chalk**
- **chalkboard**
- **three index cards**
- **marker**
- **tape**

Tip

Create a cornucopia for your seasonal display table by inviting each student to bring in one type of corn or corn product. (You might send home a list of suggestions, including unpopped popcorn, Indian corn, canned corn, cornflakes, corn chips, and so on.) Incorporate the materials as needed for the activities in this section.

Students learn the difference between the terms *horizontal* **and** *vertical* **as they graph the way people eat corn on the cob.**

Skills and Concepts: concepts of horizontal and vertical, graphing

Steps

1 Hold up an ear of corn, as though you were going to eat it. Tell students that while most people hold their corn the same way, they eat it differently. Some eat their corn by biting around (vertically) while others eat it by biting across (horizontally).

2 Introduce the terms *horizontal* and *vertical*. Provide examples by drawing lines on paper and examining objects in your room. Ask students to hold their pencils horizontally and vertically.

3 Copy a class set of graph markers and give one to each child. Ask children to decide whether they eat their corn horizontally or vertically and to record it on the marker. Students who do not eat corn can leave the graph marker blank.

4 Use your chalkboard to create a vertical graph. Label three index cards "Horizontal," "Vertical," and "I Don't Eat Corn." Draw an arrow on the first two cards to illustrate each word. Tape each card, one next to the other, to the bottom of the chalkboard.

5 Invite students to place their graph markers in the appropriate column. Ask questions to guide a discussion—for example:

- ✿ How many students eat their corn horizontally (or vertically)?
- ✿ How many eat corn all together?
- ✿ Do more students eat their corn horizontally or vertically?
- ✿ How many more students eat their corn horizontally (or vertically)?

Look What's Made From Corn!

This sorting and graphing activity introduces students to the many foods that come from corn.

Skills and Concepts: sorting and classifying; graphing

Steps

1 Fill a bag with corn and non-corn foods (one per child). Make two circles with yarn on the floor. Label one "Corn" and one "No Corn."

2 Pass around the bag and let students take turns pulling out a food item. Have students take turns sorting the food into the two circles based on whether or not the items contain corn.

3 Ask students to look closely at the items in the "No Corn" group. See if there is anybody who thinks there are items that don't belong. Check the ingredient list together to see if any items contain corn. Have students observe the "Corn" group. Ask: *Are there any items in this group that do not belong?* Check ingredients.

4 Once the items are correctly sorted, ask the following questions:

✿ How many food items contain corn?
✿ How many food items do not contain corn?
✿ Are there more or fewer food items that contain corn?
✿ How many more (or fewer) food items contain corn?

5 Remove the food items from the circles. Rearrange the yarn circles on the floor so they overlap, creating a Venn diagram. Choose two of the corn items and place one in each circle. Give each child a corn kernel. Ask children to place their kernels in the circle representing the food they like to eat. If they like both, they should place their kernel in the overlapping section. If they like neither, they should place their kernel outside of the two circles. What information they can gather from the Venn diagram? Ask:

✿ How many people like _____?
✿ How many people like both food items?
✿ How many more people like _____ than _____?

Materials

- **corn products** (such as corn-flakes, popcorn, canned corn, cornmeal, corn chips, corn tortillas, and items containing cornstarch or corn syrup)
- **non-corn food products** (such as yogurt, spaghetti sauce, canned non-corn soup, peanut butter)
- **bag**
- **yarn**
- **two index cards**
- **marker**
- **unpopped corn**

Tip

If time permits, change the food items and repeat step 5.

Feed the Ducks

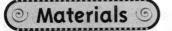
- **duck pattern** (see below)
- **construction paper**
- **glue**
- **resealable bags** (one per student)
- **10-12 pieces of unpopped corn for each student**

Explain to students that corn is food for some animals. In this activity, they'll feed ducks as they practice addition, subtraction, more and less, and equal shares.

Skills and Concepts: addition, subtraction, more and less, equal shares

Steps

1 Give each student two duck patterns. Have children glue their ducks to construction paper to make story mats.

2 Guide them in using the corn as a manipulative to find the answer to the following story problems:

✿ Feed Duck 1 three pieces of corn and Duck 2 five pieces of corn. Which duck was fed more corn? How many more pieces? (Repeat as needed, substituting different numbers.)

✿ Feed Duck 1 four pieces of corn and Duck 2 two pieces of corn. How many pieces of corn did they eat all together? Can you find a different way to show that the ducks ate six pieces of corn? (Repeat as needed, substituting different numbers.)

✿ Using eight pieces of corn, try to give Duck 1 and Duck 2 the same number of pieces (equal or fair shares). Repeat, substituting different numbers—both odd and even.

When Will It Pop?

Students learn about time as they estimate and count how long it takes popcorn to pop.

Skills and Concepts: estimation, time

Steps

1 Demonstrate for students how long a second lasts by snapping your fingers every time a second passes. Ask students if they know how many seconds equal one minute. Snap your fingers every second for a minute while they count.

2 Tell students that you are going to make some popcorn. Ask them to estimate how many seconds will pass before the first kernel pops and to record estimates on the record sheet.

3 Ask students to raise their hands if they estimated that it would take less than 60 seconds (or one minute) for the first kernel to pop. How many students estimated it would take more than 60 seconds?

4 Heat the kernels and begin counting the seconds aloud with students. At the same time, listen for the first pop.

5 After the first kernel pops, ask students how many seconds it took. Ask: *Is this more or less than one minute?* Have students record the information and compare it to their estimates. How many students had estimates that were too low? Too high? Just right?

6 If time permits, repeat the activity and compare results. Ask: *What should we do with all the popcorn we popped?* When students say "eat it," pass the bowl around and enjoy.

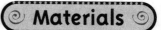

Materials

- **When Will It Pop? record sheet** (see page 16)
- **one bag of unpopped popcorn**
- **hot-air popper or stove, pan, and oil** (for adult use only)
- **butter**
- **salt**
- **bowl**

Tip

Be sure to check on food allergies before serving any food.

Kernel Count

Materials

- jar
- unpopped popcorn
- paper cups
- resealable bags
- plastic or foam bowls
- paper
- markers

Students learn about place value as they estimate and count the number of kernels in a jar.

Skills and Concepts: estimation, place value

Steps

1 Place the popcorn kernels in the jar. Ask students to estimate the number of kernels in the jar and to record their estimates.

2 Divide students into pairs. Give each pair some kernels until all kernels are distributed. Have students put each group of ten kernels into a paper cup and any leftover kernels (a group of less than ten) into the plastic bag. When all students have finished, have them bring their paper cups and plastic bags to the carpet and sit in a circle formation.

3 In the center of the circle, empty all the bags of leftover kernels on the floor. Count the kernels by ones with the students and place groups of ten kernels into paper cups. Leave leftover kernels (a group of less than ten) in a pile.

4 Count the cups by tens with students. Each time you reach 100, empty the cups of kernels into a bowl. Leave leftover cups of kernels (less than ten cups) in a cluster.

5 To determine the total number of kernels, count the groups of 100 (the bowls) with students and write the number on the left side of a piece of paper. Count the groups of ten (the paper cups) with students and write that number in the middle of the paper. Count the pile of ones (individual kernels) with students and write that number on the right side of the paper. Show students how to read the total number of kernels recorded.

6 Have students check their estimates and decide whether they are higher or lower than the actual number.

Extra, Extra...

Language Arts: COMPOUND WORDS

Write the word *popcorn* on a chart. Talk with students about how the word may have come about. *(When you heat the corn it pops and creates popcorn.)* Ask students if they can find the two words that make the word *popcorn*. Explain that *popcorn* is a compound word because it is made up of two little words. Ask students to think of other words that are compound words. Start a word wall of compound words.

Art: CORNCOB PRINTS

Collect several dried corncobs and place them at a center with paint, paper, paper towels, newspaper, and foam trays (one for each corncob). Cover the work area with newspaper and line each tray with a folded paper towel. Pour one color paint (use fall colors such as brown, yellow, red, and orange) into each tray. Invite students to visit the center and make corncob prints by dipping the cobs into the paint and rolling them on their papers. For multicolored corncob prints, let students place several colors of paint on one tray.

Music and Movement: POP POP POP

Share the following poem with your students. Whenever you say the word *pop*, invite them to pop up and down like pieces of popping corn.

POPCORN

Pop, pop, pop,
Pour corn in the pot.

Pop, pop, pop,
Shake it and shake it 'til it's hot.

Pop, pop, pop,
Open the lid and what have you got?

Pop, pop, pop,
POPCORN!

—*Author Unknown*

Literature Connections

Corn Is Maize
by Aliki (HarperTrophy, 1986). This book explains how corn was discovered by Indian farmers thousands of years ago and how it is used today.

Corn—On and Off the Cob
by Allen Fowler (Children's Press, 1995). With simple text and color photographs, this book tells about the different kinds of corn and its uses past and present.

The Popcorn Book
by Tomie DePaola (Holiday House, 1988). A little boy reads about the history of popcorn while making some for himself.

The Year of No More Corn
by Helen Ketteman (Orchard Books, 1993). Beanie has been told that he is too young to help plant corn. To comfort Beanie, Grandpa tells him a tall tale about the failure of the corn crop in 1928.

Graph Markers

I eat my corn _____.

When Will It Pop?

Name _____   Date _____

I estimate it will take ⬤ seconds for the first kernel to pop.

This is ⬤ less than ⬤ more than one minute.

It took ⬤ seconds for the first kernel to pop.

My estimate was ⬤ too low ⬤ too high ⬤ just right.

Looking at Leaves

In the blanket of leaves that covers your schoolyard lie many possibilities for exploring math. Your students will discover patterns on leafy twigs and in leaf prints they make. They'll learn about symmetry, shapes, and sizes, too!

- **Related Themes: Fall, Trees, Plants**

Patterned Prints

Students apply the concept of patterning and explore the properties of leaves through printmaking.

Skills and Concepts: creating and reading patterns

Steps

1 Demonstrate how to make a leaf print. Take a leaf and paint the underside with a brush. Place it on a strip of paper and gently press down on it. Continue modeling this process to create a pattern on the paper using leaves brushed with different colors.

2 Place a set of materials at each work space and let students create their own patterns.

3 Invite students to share their leafy patterns and let classmates describe the patterns they see.

Materials

- **different types of leaves**
- **paint** (red, yellow, orange, and brown)
- **paintbrushes**
- **paper cut in strips** (approximately 18 inches long)

Leafy Lengths

Students measure and compare leaves of different lengths.

Skills and Concepts: measuring length

Steps

1 Demonstrate how to measure the length of a leaf in inches using a ruler. Pass a few leaves and rulers around so that students can try.

2 Place five leaves at a center along with rulers and copies of the record sheet. Assign each leaf a number (1 to 5) and label them accordingly with a piece of masking tape.

3 Invite students to visit the center in small groups and measure each leaf. Have them draw pictures of their leaves and record their measurements on the record sheet. After they measure all of the leaves, have students determine and record the longest and shortest leaf.

Materials

- **leaves**
- **rulers**
- **Leafy Lengths record sheet** (see page 22)
- **marker**
- **masking tape**

Equal Sides

Students examine leaves to see if they are symmetrical.

Skills and Concepts: measurement, equal, symmetry

Steps

1 Demonstrate the concept of symmetry by folding a leaf in half. Explain to students that if the edges of both sides match, the leaf is symmetrical. If they don't, the leaf is not.

2 Give each student a leaf. Have students fold their leaves in half, then check to see if the edges match.

3 Ask students who have symmetrical leaves to hold them up. Let students visit with one another to see the symmetry in different leaves. Have students exchange leaves and repeat the activity.

Materials

- **leaves**

Leaf Lineup

Students practice reading and extending patterns while investigating alternate, opposite and whorled leaf patterns.

Skills and Concepts: reading patterns, extending patterns

Steps

1 After a rainy or windy day, collect leafy twigs. Gather students in a circle and pass around the twigs. Ask students to pay close attention to the leaves. Can they see patterns in the way the leaves grow on the twigs?

2 Begin drawing one of the leaf patterns on the chalkboard. Once you've drawn enough leaves to establish the pattern, invite a volunteer to draw the next leaf and describe the pattern. Continue, allowing students to take turns adding leaves to the pattern.

3 Give each child a copy of "Leaf Lineup." Ask students to find the pattern that matches the one they drew on the board. Name the pattern and ask students to extend it by drawing more leaves.

4 Next, draw students' attention to the two remaining leaf patterns on the paper. Ask them to describe and compare these patterns. Name the patterns and ask students to extend them by drawing more leaves.

5 As a follow-up, provide each student with six spearmint leaf gumdrops and one licorice or pretzel stick. Ask them to create leaf patterns using these materials.

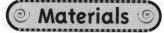

Materials

- leafy twigs
- chalkboard
- chalk
- **Leaf Lineup activity sheet** (see page 23)
- pencils
- six spearmint leaf gumdrops for each student
- one licorice or pretzel stick for each student

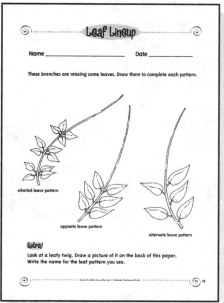

19

Taking Up Space

⊙ Materials ⊙

- **cardboard**
- **scissors**
- **an outdoor area with fallen leaves**

Challenge students to a scavenger hunt where they'll search for leaves in different shapes and sizes.

Skills and Concepts: area, length, width

Steps

1 Cut the cardboard into square and rectangular shapes that are approximately the size (length and width) of leaves around your school.

2 Take students outdoors to an area with lots of fallen leaves. Give them each a cardboard shape and ask them to find a leaf that "just about" fills that space. The leaf should be as long and as wide (at its longest and widest parts) as the cardboard shape.

3 When students think they have found a match, ask them to show it to you. Once you've checked their work, give them a different cardboard shape and let them repeat the activity.

⊙Tip

Learn more about leaves with *First Field Guides: Trees* (Scholastic, 1999). This easy-to-use guide contains facts, photographs, and illustrations for more than 150 trees, including 50 that are likely to be found in North America. A water-resistant "spotter's card" makes it easy to identify trees in the field.

Extra, Extra...

Literature Connections

Music and Movement: FALLING LEAVES

Invite students to move like the leaves in the following poem as you read it aloud. For a variation, let one student be the wind, moving quickly through the other students and causing them to whirl and twirl around. Give each child a copy of the poem to take home. (See page 24.) Encourage children to repeat the activity as a family member reads the poem.

FALLING LEAVES

Little leaves fall softly down,
Red and yellow, orange and brown,
Whirling, twirling round and round,
Falling softly to the ground.

Little leaves fall softly down
To make a carpet on the ground.
Then swish, the wind comes whistling by
And sends them dancing to the sky.

—*Author Unknown*

Science and Nature: EDIBLE LEAVES

Ask students if they can eat leaves. Surprise them by bringing in edible leaves such as kale, spinach, lettuce, parsley, collards, mustard greens, and brussels sprouts to share with students.

Safety Tip: *Be sure to check on allergies before serving any food.*

Game: CONCENTRATION

Collect ten pairs of different kinds of leaves. Glue each leaf to a piece of cardboard and press them between two sheets of clear contact paper. Place leaf cards at a center and let students use them to play Concentration.

I Eat Leaves

by Joann Vandine (Mondo Publishing, 1995). This book introduces readers to some of the many leaf-eating animals. Your students may be surprised to find out that they are among these animals!

Look What I Did With a Leaf

by Morteza E. Sohi (Walker and Company, 1995). Full-color photographs and simple text show children how to choose and arrange leaves to create animals and scenes. Also included is a field guide for identifying leaves.

Red Leaf, Yellow Leaf

by Lois Ehlert (Harcourt Brace, 1991). Bold collage illustrations and the voice of a young child tell the story of a sugar maple tree's life cycle.

Why Do Leaves Change Color?

by Betsy Maestro (HarperCollins, 1994). The process of how leaves change color is explained in simple sentences. Includes helpful hints on making leaf rubbings and pressed leaves.

Leafy Lengths

Name _____   Date _____

Leaves	My Measurements
Leaf 1	
Leaf 2	
Leaf 3	
Leaf 4	
Leaf 5	

Which leaf is longest? _____

Which leaf is shortest? _____

Hands-On Math Around the Year • Scholastic Professional Books

Name _____   Date _____

These branches are missing some leaves. Draw them to complete each pattern.

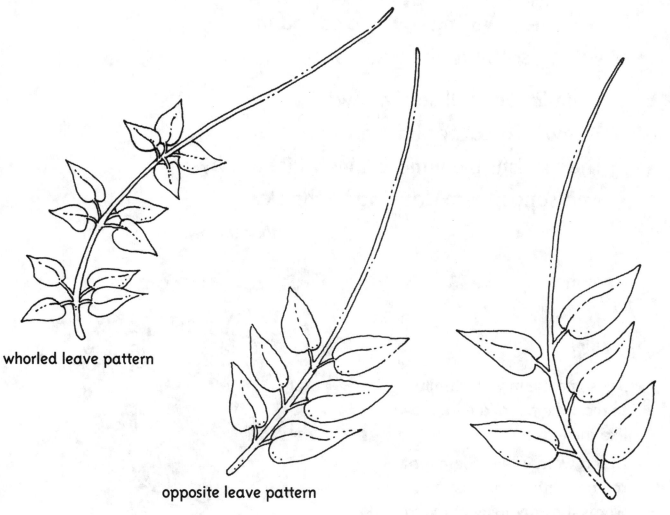

whorled leave pattern

opposite leave pattern

alternate leave pattern

Extra!

Look at a leafy twig. Draw a picture of it on the back of this paper.
Write the name for the leaf pattern you see.

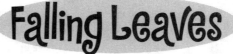

Name _____   Date _____

FALLING LEAVES

Little leaves fall softly down,
Red and yellow, orange and brown,
Whirling, twirling round and round,
Falling softly to the ground.

Little leaves fall softly down
To make a carpet on the ground.
Then swish, the wind comes whistling by
And sends them dancing to the sky.

—Author Unkown

Try This!

- Ask someone in your family to read the poem aloud. Move like the leaves!

- Find a word in the poem that rhymes with *round*. List more words that rhyme with *round*.

_____

_____

_____

_____

_____

A Patch of Pumpkins

On your next visit to the pumpkin patch (or market), bring back a few pumpkins. They're a great tool for teaching mathematics because they come in a variety of shapes and sizes and are filled with natural manipulatives—seeds! Use them for sorting, measuring, graphing, and more. Make paper pumpkins to use with a counting rhyme that students will enjoy long after the real pumpkins are gone.

● **Related Themes: Fall, Plants, Halloween**

Odd Seed Out

Teach students a strategy for determining whether a set of objects is odd or even.

Skills and Concepts: odd and even numbers

Steps

1 Demonstrate for students how to determine whether a group of objects is odd or even by taking a random number of seeds and arranging them in pairs. Tell students that if there is an "odd man out" (a leftover seed without a partner), then the number of seeds is odd, but if all the seeds have partners, then the number of seeds is even. Repeat the demonstration with different numbers of seeds.

2 Place varying numbers of seeds in ten paper cups and place them at a center.

3 Invite students to visit the center and determine whether the number of seeds in each cup is odd or even, using the strategy introduced.

Materials

● **dried pumpkin seeds**
● **ten paper cups**

Seed Toss

Students use pumpkin seeds as two-color counters to practice reading and writing addition number sentences.

Skills and Concepts: addition, recording number sentences, number combinations

Steps

1 Lay the pumpkin seeds on newspaper. Spray paint one side of the seeds in an open area. Allow to dry overnight.

2 Give each student a Seed Toss record sheet. Have students count out pumpkin seeds based on a number you identify. For example, if you're exploring number combinations that add up to seven, you'll want each student to take seven seeds.

3 Demonstrate how to place the seeds in a cup, shake them, and spill them onto a table or desk.

4 Model for students how to count the seeds. Count the number of orange seeds and the number of white seeds. Record the numbers on a copy of the record sheet. For example, if you spill the seeds and five are orange and two are white, you will record this as $5 + 2 = 7$.

5 Direct students to toss their seeds ten times, recording the number sentence on the Seed Toss record sheet each time.

6 Ask students to share the different number combinations they found using the same number of seeds. Record them on the chalkboard. How many different combinations did students discover?

7 Give students a different number of seeds and repeat the activity.

Materials

- **dried pumpkin seeds**
- **orange spray paint**
- **newspaper**
- **Seed Toss record sheet** (see page 31)
- **paper cups**
- **pencils**

Tip

Gather pumpkins in assorted sizes. Before you scoop the seeds out of a medium-size pumpkin, invite students to estimate the number of seeds. Cut open the pumpkin, remove the seeds, and let students count them out in groups of ten. Add up the tens and ones to get the total. Rinse the seeds, let them dry overnight on newspaper, and your seed counters will be ready for use.

Squashed

Students examine and sort squash—including pumpkins!

Skills and Concepts: sorting and classifying

Steps

1 Gather students in a circle. Place the squashes in the center of the circle.

2 Share with students the name of each squash. Let students describe properties of the squash, including size, shape, color, and texture. Pass each one around so students can take a closer look.

3 Sort squashes by color without saying anything. Place a piece of string around each group to separate one from another. Ask students to guess your sorting rule.

4 Let a student sort the squashes using a different sorting rule. Let remaining students guess the rule. Continue, letting students take turns sorting and guessing.

5 Discuss what makes a pumpkin like other squash. Cut open the squashes so that students can make other comparisons.

6 Give each child a pumpkin pattern. Ask children to write a word on the pattern that describes pumpkin or other squash. Display the pumpkin patterns to make a word wall. Make blank pumpkin patterns available so students can add new words.

Materials

- **several different kinds of squash** (such as acorn and butternut; include a pumpkin)
- **string**
- **scissors**
- **pumpkin pattern** (see below)

Pumpkin Pounds

 **Materials**

- **five pumpkins**
  (varying sizes)
- **pumpkin pattern**
  (see page 27)
- **tape**
- **bathroom scale**

Students explore weight as they predict which pumpkin is heaviest, then test their predictions and graph results.

Skills and Concepts: estimation of weight, measurement of weight, graphing

Steps

1 Label the pumpkins with numbers one to five. Give each child a pumpkin pattern. Ask students to predict which will be the heaviest and to write that pumpkin's number on their pumpkin pattern.

2 Make a graph on the chalkboard using the pumpkin patterns by taping all the ones in one column, twos in another column, and so on.

3 Discuss the graph by asking the following questions:

✿ How many students think pumpkin number one will be the heaviest? (Continue with pumpkins two through five.)

✿ Which pumpkin do most students think is the heaviest?

4 Weigh each pumpkin using the bathroom scale. Place pumpkins in order according to weight.

5 Compare results to the graph. Did most students guess correctly? If not, discuss why one pumpkin looked heavier than the others, but wasn't.

6 Share this bit of pumpkin trivia: The largest pumpkin ever grown (at the time this book was printed) was 821 pounds and was big enough to make 400 pumpkin pies!

Ten Little Pumpkins

Students create a paper prop to go with a traditional counting rhyme.

Skills and Concepts: subtraction, recording number sentences

Steps

1 Cut out ten orange felt or construction paper pumpkins using the pumpkin pattern as a template. Place the pumpkins on a feltboard or attach them to a bulletin board or chalkboard.

2 Read aloud the rhyme. Remove a pumpkin each time one disappears in the poem. Share the rhyme a second time, stopping after each stanza to write the corresponding subtraction number sentence.

3 Guide students in following these directions to make accordion-fold pumpkins to go with the rhyme.

❀ Fold a sheet of orange construction paper in half horizontally.

❀ Make four 2-inch accordion folds from left to right.

❀ Draw a pumpkin on the folded paper, making sure that the left and right sides of the pumpkin extend to the sides of the paper. Cut out the pumpkin, leaving the sides intact (so the pumpkins will stay joined together when the paper is unfolded).

4 Have students open up their folded sheets of paper. They will be surprised to find two strips of five pumpkins each. Have students tape the two strips together to create "ten little pumpkins."

5 Share the rhyme a third time. As each pumpkin disappears, have students fold their strips so that one fewer pumpkin is showing.

6 Let students use their accordion-fold pumpkins to make and solve subtraction problems. For example, write 6 - 2 = _____ on the chalkboard. Have students fold their pumpkins so only six are showing. Have them take away two more. How many are left?

Materials

- **pumpkin pattern** (see page 27)
- **orange felt or paper**
- **feltboard**
- **"Ten Little Pumpkins" poem** (see page 32)
- **9-by-12-inch orange paper**
- **tape**

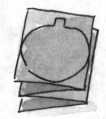

Literature Connections

Big Pumpkin

by Erica Silverman (Aladdin Paperbacks, 1995). In this cumulative tale, a witch plants a pumpkin seed and the pumpkin grows, and grows, and grows until at last it is too heavy to lift. One by one, other Halloween characters come to her aid in trying to move the "big pumpkin."

It's Pumpkin Time

by Zoe Hall (Scholastic Trade, 1996). Simple text and bold illustrations tell the story of a brother and sister who work together to create a jack-o'-lantern patch.

Pumpkin, Pumpkin

by Jeanne Titherington (Mulberry Books, 1990). A simple story, told in one sentence, of a boy planting a pumpkin seed and watching it grow.

The Biggest Pumpkin Ever

by Steven Kroll (Cartwheel Books, 1993). Two mice fall in love with the same pumpkin, but for different reasons.

Extra, Extra...

Snack: TOASTED PUMPKIN SEEDS

Cut open a pumpkin and remove the seeds. Rinse them thoroughly and let them dry on a paper towel for a day or so. Put one tablespoon of cooking oil and the dried seeds into a bowl. Mix until the seeds are well coated. Spread the seeds on a cookie sheet and bake at 350° Fahrenheit for 45 minutes.

Safety Tip: *Be sure to check on allergies before serving any food.*

Game: PUMPKIN TOSS

Paint the numbers 10, 20, 30, and 40 on four pumpkins. Arrange them in a line from low to high, with pumpkins about twelve inches apart. Let students take turns tossing a hula hoop around a pumpkin. How many tosses will it take before the class reaches 100 points?

Health: PUT ON A PUMPKIN FACE

Decorate several pumpkins so that each one expresses a different emotion—for example, sad, happy, angry, and so on. Display the pumpkins and ask students how each is feeling. Discuss times they've had those feelings. Give students orange construction paper and let them cut out pumpkin shapes. Have them color the pumpkins to show how they're feeling that day.

Seed Toss

Name _____   Date _____

Orange Seeds		White Seeds		Total
1. _____	+	_____	=	_____
2. _____	+	_____	=	_____
3. _____	+	_____	=	_____
4. _____	+	_____	=	_____
5. _____	+	_____	=	_____
6. _____	+	_____	=	_____
7. _____	+	_____	=	_____
8. _____	+	_____	=	_____
9. _____	+	_____	=	_____
10. _____	+	_____	=	_____

Name _____ Date _____

TEN LITTLE PUMPKINS

Ten little pumpkins
All in a line,
One became a jack-o'-lantern,
Then there were nine.

Nine little pumpkins
Peeking through the gate,
An old witch took one,
Then there were eight.

Eight little pumpkins
(There never were eleven),
A green goblin took one,
Then there were seven.

Seven little pumpkins
Full of jolly tricks,
A white ghost took one,
Then there were six.

Six little pumpkins
Glad to be alive,
A black cat took one,
Then there were five.

Five little pumpkins
By the barn door,
A hoot owl took one,
Then there were four.

Four little pumpkins
(As you can plainly see),
One became a pumpkin pie,
Then there were three.

Three little pumpkins
Feeling very blue,
One rolled far away,
Then there were two.

Two little pumpkins
Alone in the sun,
One said, "So long,"
And then there was one.

One little pumpkin
Left all alone,
A little boy chose him,
Then there were none.

Ten little pumpkins
In a patch so green
Made everyone happy
On Halloween.

—*Author Unknown*

All About Apples

Y ou'll get a lot of mileage out of apples as a teaching tool when you work with them in bits and pieces. The stem is the first part to go as students estimate, count, and graph the number of turns it takes to separate it from the apple. Apples cut in halves, thirds, and quarters invite activities in counting, fractions, and more.

● **Related Themes: Fall, Trees, Plants, Fruits**

Stems Away

Students create a number line to show how many twists it takes for apple stems to fall off.

Skills and Concepts: numerical order, creating a number line, graphing

Steps

1 Give each student an apple and an apple pattern. Ask students to hold the stem with one hand and turn the apple with the other, counting each turn until the stem breaks off. Have students record the number of turns on the apple patterns.

2 Create an incomplete number line by writing "1" at the left end of the chalkboard, "5" in the middle, and "10" at the right end. Let students take turns taping their apple patterns in the correct position on the number line.

3 Use the number line for more math—for example, ask: *What number shows the fewest turns? What number shows the most turns?*

◎ Materials ◎

- **apples** (one per student)
- **apple pattern** (see page 39)
- **tape**

Way Up High

Students listen to a traditional counting rhyme and follow along using a math story mat and manipulatives.

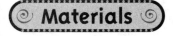
Skills and Concepts:
addition, subtraction

Steps

1 Record the following rhyme on a piece of chart paper:

WAY UP HIGH

Way up high in the apple tree
Ten little apples smiled at me.
I shook that tree as hard as I could
And one fell down.
Mmm good!
(Repeat until no apples are left on the tree.)

—*Traditional*

Tip

Use the story mat and red hots (apples) as manipulatives for other addition and subtraction story problems.

2 Share the rhyme several times with students so they become familiar with it. Give each student a copy of the apple tree story mat and ten cinnamon red hots. Recite the rhyme once more with students and have them manipulate the red hots (apples) to go along with the rhyme.

3 Give each child a copy of page 41. Have children cut out the apple shape and use it to trace and cut out ten more apples. Ask them to write each additional verse of the poem (for numbers nine through one, and the last verse in which no apples are left) on an apple. Have children put their pages in order and staple to make a book.

4 Let children take home their mini-books, story mats, and red hots to share with their families.

Apple Addition

Students make sets of apple prints and write number sentences to go with them.

Skills and Concepts: addition, recording number sentences

Steps

1 Prepare for this activity by covering the desks or work area with newspaper and pouring the paint in the foam trays.

2 Demonstrate how to dip an apple into the paint, blot it on the paper towel, and stamp it onto the paper.

3 After making a few apple prints of each color, show students how to write the number sentence that corresponds to the apple prints (for example, $4 + 3 = 7$).

4 Cover a center with newspaper and stock it with apples, paint, and paper.

5 Invite students to make their own apple prints and write the number sentences to go with them.

- newspaper
- paint
- two foam trays
- one apple cut in half
- paper towels
- large sheets of paper

Appleseed Counting Book

Do all apples have the same number of seeds? Students make mini-books to show the answer.

Skills and Concepts: counting 1 to 10, writing numerals

Steps

1 Ask students if they think all apples have the same number of seeds.

2 Take one apple, cut it in half, and count the number of seeds together. Do the same with the other apples.

3 After students realize that apples contain varying numbers of seeds, allow them to create seed counting books.

4 Cover the desks or work area with newspaper. Show students how to dip an apple into the paint, blot it on the paper towel, and stamp it on the paper.

5 Have students make eleven apple prints, one on each page.

6 When the paint is dry, have students draw seeds on the apples. On pages 1 to 10, have them draw first one seed, then two, then three, and so on, to create a counting book. Students can make a cover with the remaining apple print, adding as many seeds as they like.

7 Have students color stems on the apples and add any other finishing touches. Then have them put their pages in order and write the corresponding numerals 1 to 10.

8 Help students bind their books using paper fasteners, staples, or yarn.

Materials

- **four apples**
- **knife** (for adult use only)
- **newspaper**
- **red, yellow, or green paint**
- **one foam tray**
- **paper towels**
- **black and green markers or crayons**
- **8 1/2-by-11-inch paper** (11 sheets per student)
- **paper fasteners, staples, or yarn**

Tip

As a variation, make counting books for skip counting by twos, fives, tens, and so on.

The Fractions Game

Students suggest ways to share an apple as they play a fractions game.

Skills and Concepts: fractions

Steps

1 Take the first apple and ask students how two people could share it. Cut the apple in half.

2 Take the second apple and ask students how three people could share it. Cut the apple in thirds.

3 Take the third apple and ask students how four people could share it. Cut the apple in fourths.

4 Give each student a copy of The Fractions Game and provide the following instructions for play:

✿ Each player takes turns rolling the die.

✿ The number that appears on the die indicates the number of slices the player can color in on any of the apples.

✿ The winner is the one who colors in all the slices on all the apples first.

- **three apples**
- **knife** (for adult use only)
- **The Fractions Game** (see page 42)
- **crayons**
- **dice**

Extra, Extra...

Applesauce

by Shirley Kurtz (Good Books, 1992). Join a family in making and canning applesauce. The back of the book contains specific directions, should you want to try it with your students.

How Do Apples Grow?

by Betsy Maestro (HarperTrophy, 1993). Learn about the life cycle of an apple tree and the different parts of an apple plant.

Real Stuck Way Up

by Bennette Tiffault (Barron Books, 1995). This cumulative tale tells of a boy who throws many objects into a tree to try and free an apple that is stuck— real stuck way up.

The Seasons of Arnold's Apple Tree

by Gail Gibbons (Harcourt Brace, 1988). Arnold enjoys his apple tree through the seasons. The book includes a recipe for apple pie and a diagram showing how a cider press works.

Snack: NO-COOK APPLESAUCE

Here's an easy way to make applesauce with your students. You'll need one apple and two teaspoons of honey for every two students.

- Peel and core the apples. Cut them into quarters and chop into small chunks.
- Place the chunks in a blender and add honey. Blend the mixture until smooth.
- Pour into serving dishes and sprinkle with cinnamon.

Safety Tip: *Be sure to check on allergies before serving any food.*

Social Studies: WHERE DO APPLES GROW?

Tell students that apples grow best in areas where winters are moderately cool and summers are made up of warm days and cool nights. Display a U.S. map. Can students guess which states are known for growing apples? (*California, New York, North Carolina, Michigan, Pennsylvania, and Washington*)

Science and Nature: AN APPLE EXPERIMENT

Try this experiment with your students. Take three pieces of apple and place each one on a paper towel. Write "water" on one towel, "lemon" on another, and "nothing" on the last. Pour water on the first piece, squeeze lemon on the next, and do nothing to the third one. Wait one hour and look at the apple pieces. Ask students to describe how they've changed. Check again after two more hours.
Discuss the results.

Name _____

It took _____ twists for my apple's stem to fall off.

Apple Tree Story Mat

Name _____ **Date** _____

Hands-On Math Around the Year • Scholastic Professional Books

Name _____   Date _____

✿ Cut out the apple. Trace ten more apples. Cut out each apple.

✿ Write each new verse of the poem on an apple. (Way up high in the apple tree, nine little apples smiled at me; then eight; and so on.)

✿ Put your apples in order. Staple the apples to make a book.

Way Up High

Way up high in the apple tree

Ten little apples smiled at me.

I shook that tree as hard as I could

And one fell down.

Mmm good!

The Fractions Game

Name _____   Date _____

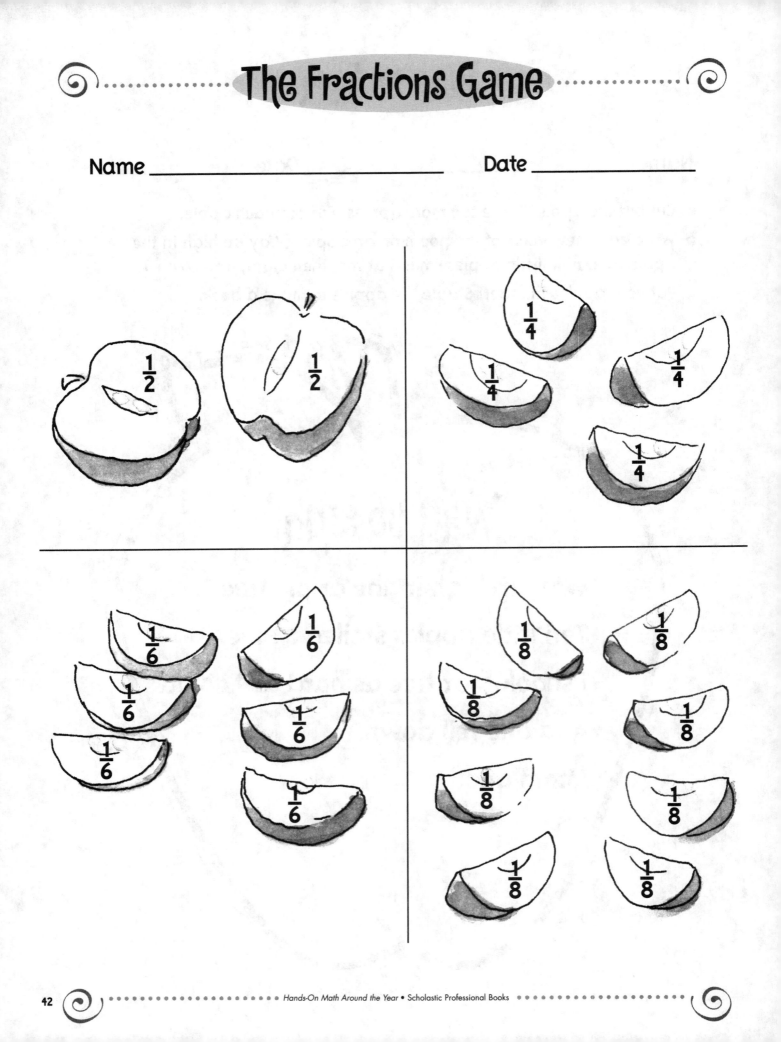

Exploring Nuts & Cones

Long after trees have left them behind, nuts and cones make wonderful math manipulatives. Nuts make great counters because they are available in large quantities and are relatively uniform in size. Cones come in many sizes and make an interesting non-standard set of weights. Use them to practice one-to-one correspondence, estimate and measure surface area, and explore concepts of sinking and floating.

- **Related Themes: Trees, Plants, Seeds**

How Many Nuts?

Students use nuts to measure the surface area of a circle.

Skills and Concepts: surface area, counting by ones

Materials

- **assorted nuts**
  (four kinds)
- **four containers**
- **How Many Nuts?**
  record sheet
  (see page 49)

Steps

1 Place nuts in the containers by type. Label the containers 1 to 4. Place copies of the How Many Nuts? record sheet and the nuts at a center.

2 Invite students to visit the center and, beginning with container 1, estimate how many nuts it will take to fill the circle on their record sheet. Have them write their estimate in the space for container 1.

3 Have students fill the surface area of the circle with nuts from container 1. Ask them count the number of nuts it took to fill in the circle, and record this information. Have students repeat steps 2 and 3 for the other three containers of nuts.

4 Bring students together to compare results. How close were their counts for each container?

Do Pinecones Float?

In an attempt to answer this question, students make predictions, test them, and graph results.

Skills and Concepts: graphing

Steps

1 Make a floor graph by drawing two columns and approximately 20 rows on a piece of chart paper or posterboard. Label the columns "sink" and "float."

2 Ask students to predict whether they think pinecones will sink or float and to record their predictions on the floor graph using a small pinecone as a marker.

3 Gather students around the floor graph and ask the following questions:

- ✿ How many students think pinecones will sink?
- ✿ How many students think pinecones will float?
- ✿ Do more students think pinecones will float or sink?
- ✿ How many students participated in the graph all together?
- ✿ How can we find out if pinecones sink or float?

4 Gather students around the tub of water. Place one pinecone in the tub. Once students see that it floats, show them a different pinecone and ask if they think this one will float, too. Continue testing all six pinecones until students are convinced that all pinecones float.

5 Discuss with students reasons why the pinecones floated. Break one open and show students the air spaces inside.

Materials

- **chart paper or posterboard**
- **marker**
- **small pinecones** (one per student)
- **plastic dish tub**
- **water**
- **six pinecones** (varying types and sizes)

Tip

Explain to students that both nuts and cones provide shelter for seeds. Demonstrate this by shaking out the seeds from a cone or cracking open a nut. Invite students to bring in several nuts or cones from home. You may also want to purchase a bag of nuts from the grocery store. If necessary, you can also purchase pinecones in most craft shops.

Oh Nuts!

Students help squirrels gather nuts, then divide them equally to learn more.

Skills and Concepts: one-to-one correspondence, concept of subtraction

Steps

1 Ask students if they know what squirrels do in the fall. Explain that the nuts they hide so they will have food to eat in the winter is called a *cache*. When winter comes, sometimes squirrels don't remember where their cache is hidden or find that other animals have discovered it and claimed it as their own.

2 To prepare for this activity, hide eight nuts somewhere in the classroom. Make a transparency from the Oh Nuts! reproducible (see page 50) and place it on the overhead. Tell students that the squirrels in the circle can't find their store of nuts and need their help. Send students on a search for the nuts in the classroom.

3 When students find all the nuts, have them match them one-to-one with the squirrels on the overhead. Place the two extra nuts outside the circle. Ask:

❀ Are there more squirrels or more nuts? How do you know?
❀ How many more nuts are there than squirrels? How do you know?

4 Repeat the activity using a different number of nuts.

5 Give each student a cup of ten nuts and a copy of Oh Nuts! Provide students with practice on one-to-one correspondence by telling them to take different numbers of nuts out of their cups and match them to the squirrels. Repeat the questions in step 3.

Materials

- **Oh Nuts!** (see page 50)
- **nuts** (any kind; ten per student; extras for hiding)
- **paper cups** (one per student)

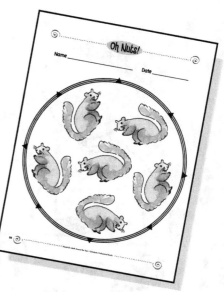

45

Two of a Kind

Materials

- **20-30 pinecones** (assorted types and sizes)
- **balance scale**

Students investigate weight using different-size cones and a balance scale.

Skills and Concepts: weight

Steps

1 Gather students in a circle. Place the scale and pinecones in the center.

2 Invite a student to choose a pinecone and place it in one of the pans on the balance scale.

3 Ask students to search with their eyes for another pinecone that looks as if it might weigh about the same as the one already in the pan.

4 Experiment with several pinecones until you find one that will balance the scale.

5 Repeat this process using other pinecones. When there is no match, demonstrate for students how several small pinecones together can weigh the same as a larger one.

6 Place the pinecones and balance scale at a center. Let students spend time on their own trying to balance the scale.

A Nutty Game

Children get practice dividing objects equally with this activity.

Skills and Concepts: equal shares

Steps

- **tagboard**
- **pencils**
- **nuts** (one bag or bowl per group)

1 Divide the class into groups of four. Provide each group with a sheet of tagboard, pencils, and a bag or bowl of nuts. Guide students in using the tagboard to create a game board, as shown below. Have them draw a large circle in the center, and write the numbers 1, 2, 3, 4, in the corners (one number per corner).

2 Have each group member choose a number on the game board and place his or her initials next to it.

3 To play, have each group select a player to go first. This player takes a handful of nuts and places them in the center of the game board. He or she then divides the nuts among the players, placing them in the corners of the paper.

4 If the nuts can be divided into four equal shares, the student whose number comes after the first player's number takes the next turn.

5 If the nuts cannot be divided equally, the extras are left in the center. The winner is the person whose number matches the number of nuts remaining.

6 This game can be played over and over again with students keeping a tally of the number of times they win.

Literature Connections

Nuts (Would You Believe It)

by Catherine Chambers (Raintree/Steck Vaughn, 1996). Simple language and photographs show how nuts are used throughout the world.

Squirrel Is Hungry

by Satoshi Kitamura (Farrar, Straus & Giroux, 1996). Where will Squirrel keep his walnut? He tries putting it in a bird's nest, under a rock, and in the hollow of a tree before he finds the perfect spot.

Extra, Extra...

Art: PINECONE PAINTING

Place paint, pinecones, paper, and a plastic tub at a center. Let students follow these steps to make pinecone paintings.

- Line the bottom of the plastic tub with a blank sheet of paper.

- Place the paint-covered pinecone inside the tub.

- Move the tub from side to side so that the cone rolls all over the paper. Repeat the process using cones dipped in different colors of paint.

(You can also try this activity with nuts.)

Snack: PINE NUTS

Find a pinecone that still has seeds inside. Shake it over a black piece of paper so students can see the seeds it contains. Tell them that a pinecone is a nursery for seeds. Explain that these are called *pine nuts* and that some pine nuts are edible. Share pine nuts that you've purchased and let students taste a few. (Be sure to tell students they should never eat seeds they find outside.)

Language Arts: THE NUTCRACKER

Read a version of *The Nutcracker* to your students and play some of the music from the ballet. Bring in a nutcracker and let students take turns trying to crack a nut. Culminate the activity with a nut-tasting party.

Safety Tip: *Be sure to check on allergies before serving any food.*

Science and Nature: FOR THE BIRDS

Students can make pinecone bird feeders for their feathered friends. Give each student a pinecone. Assist them in tying string around the middle of it, leaving enough length to hang it from a branch. Pass out peanut butter and let students smear it over their pinecones using their fingers. Place birdseed in a plastic dish tub and have students roll their pinecones in it. Wrap the bird feeders in foil or plastic wrap for safe travel home.

How Many Nuts?

Name _____ Date _____

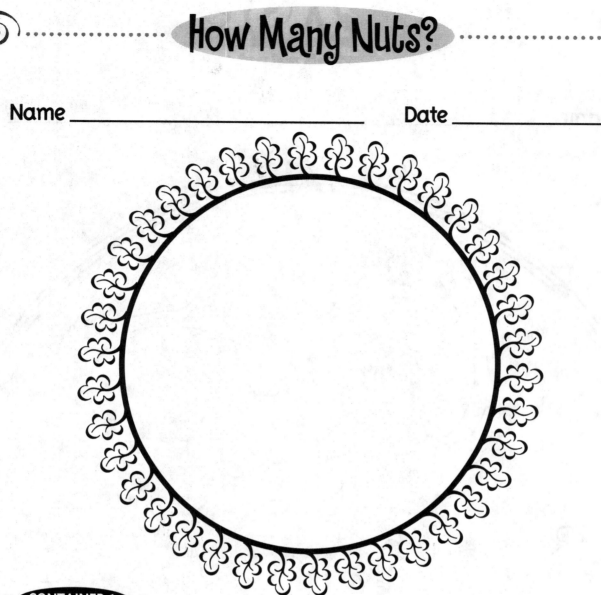

CONTAINER 1:

My Estimate: This is how many nuts I think it will take to fill the circle. _____
My Count: It took _____ nuts to fill the circle.

CONTAINER 2:

My Estimate: This is how many nuts I think it will take to fill the circle. _____
My Count: It took _____ nuts to fill the circle.

CONTAINER 3:

My Estimate: This is how many nuts I think it will take to fill the circle. _____
My Count: It took _____ nuts to fill the circle.

CONTAINER 4:

My Estimate: This is how many nuts I think it will take to fill the circle. _____
My Count: It took _____ nuts to fill the circle.

Name _____ Date _____

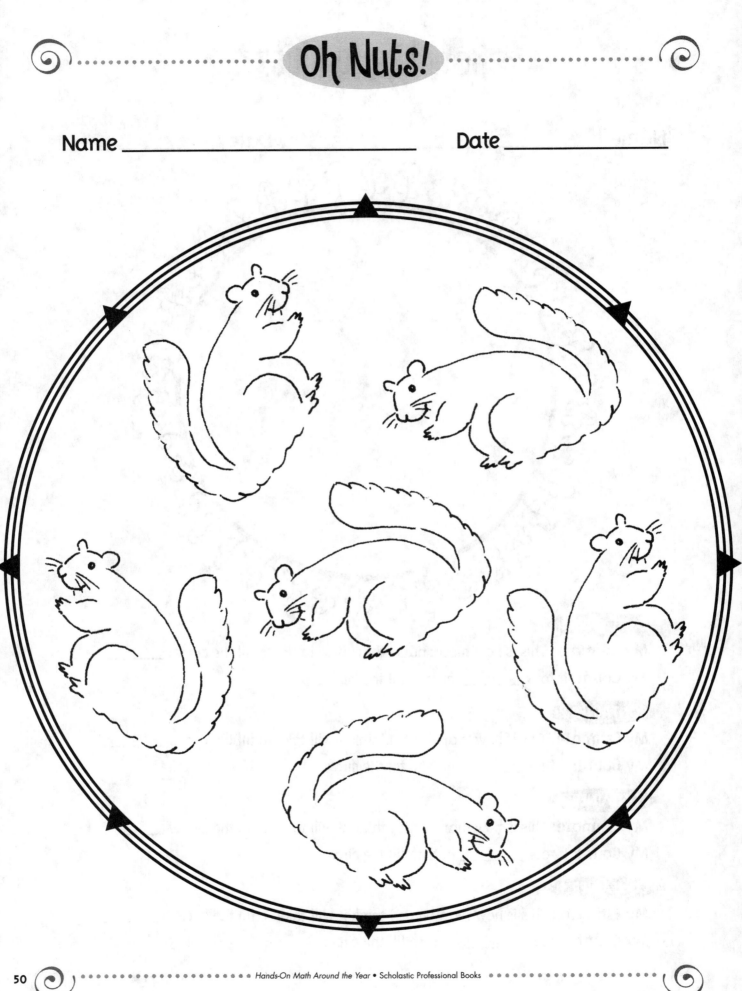

Five, Six, Pick Up Sticks

Pick up some sticks from the ground and add a twig collection to your teaching toolbox. You can find sticks in assorted lengths or customize them to meet your needs. The activities in this section invite students to use sticks to measure objects, create shapes, represent tally marks, tap out patterns, and more.

- **Related Themes: Trees, Plants, Winter**

Stick Figures

Students examine the characteristics of basic shapes.

Skills and Concepts: geometry

Steps

1 Cut a square, circle, triangle, and rectangle from construction paper. Ask students to describe the shapes. Help them recognize key character- istics—for example, the rectangle has two sides that are the same length and two more that are the same length but different from the first two.

2 Guide students in breaking their sticks to the appropriate length to create a rectangle, square, and triangle. Discuss the number and comparative sizes of the sticks they need to make each shape. Ask students how many sides a circle has. (*none*) Discuss why it would be impossible to create a circle using the sticks.

3 Place the sticks at a center. Let students use them (this time without breaking them) to create different shapes.

- **construction paper**
- **sticks** (four per student; varying lengths)

A Foot Long

Materials

- **sticks** (longer than 1 foot; one per child)
- **masking tape**
- **rulers**
- **A Foot Long record sheet** (see page 56)

Tip

The best time to collect sticks or twigs is on a windy day or after a storm. You can substitute craft sticks for twigs in Twig Tally and Tap a Pattern.

How long is a foot? Students estimate the one-foot mark on a stick, then measure objects to find out if they are shorter than, longer than, or the same as a foot.

Skills and Concepts: estimation and measurement of length

Steps

1 Ask students to estimate how long a foot is and to mark that point on their stick with a piece of masking tape.

2 Give students a ruler and have them check their estimates by measuring the stick.

3 Ask students to tell you how close their estimates were in inches—for example, *I was two inches off.* Ask students to break off their sticks at the one-foot mark.

4 Provide students with time to explore the classroom searching for objects that are longer than, shorter than, and the same as their "stick foot." Have them record their findings on their chart.

Twig Tally

Students learn to represent numerals using tally marks.

Skills and Concepts: collecting and representing data

Materials

- **20 twigs**
- **index cards**
- **marker**

Steps

1 Gather students in a circle. Lay the twigs (one at a time) on the floor in the center of the circle. Position them vertically (side by side) and invite students to count them aloud with you.

2 When you get to the fifth twig, place it across the four others, as you would when recording tally marks. Stop counting and ask students to tell you what they notice about the fifth twig.

3 Continue adding other twigs, placing every fifth one across the four previous. When you reach 20, stop and ask students if they notice a pattern.

4 Tell students that these twigs represent tally marks and that people often draw them on paper to help them keep track of a running total—for example, points scored during a game. Demonstrate this by drawing tally marks on the board to represent the number of days that have passed in the month and/or the number of students in the class-room. Provide other examples if necessary.

5 Use the twigs as tally marks to represent a number from 1 to 20. Ask students to tell you the number. Repeat the process to provide additional practice.

6 Place 20 twigs and index cards labeled with numbers 1 to 20 at a center. Invite students to visit the center and choose a number card. Using the twigs, have students represent the number in the form of tally marks.

Tap a Pattern

Materials

- *Max Found Two Sticks* by Jerry Pinkney (Simon & Schuster, 1994)
- **sticks** (two per student and two extra)

In this activity, students use sticks to imitate and create simple musical patterns.

Skills and Concepts: extending a pattern, creating a pattern, reading a pattern

Steps

1 Read *Max Found Two Sticks*, the story of a young boy who learns how to express himself using a pair of sticks.

2 As a follow-up, gather students in a circle on the floor and provide them with two sticks each. Using your own set, create a simple musical pattern by tapping one stick on top of the other. Invite students to join in. Continue tapping the pattern until all have caught on.

3 Next, without saying a word, change the pattern and continue tapping it until all students have followed your lead. Repeat this step several more times. Discuss how communication took place without any words.

4 To allow students to create their own patterns, arrange them in pairs and let them take turns tapping out a pattern for their partner to follow.

5 Gather students together again and tell them you are going to show them how to name a pattern using words or sounds. Demonstrate this with a pattern a student has tapped out— for example, "This pattern sounds like *sh, sh, boom; sh, sh, boom,*" or "I hear *red, red, blue; red, red, blue.*" Model several examples and allow students to share their own ideas for naming the patterns. Help students to see that they all heard the same pattern but named it differently. Repeat the process using patterns students tap out.

Extra, Extra...

Science and Nature: FROM BUD TO LEAF

Gather twigs from an oak tree. (Horse chestnut, forsythia, and magnolia twigs will also work.) Show students the cluster of buds at the end of a twig. Can they guess what these little bumps on the twigs are? Explain that these buds are the beginnings of next year's leaves (or flowers). Place the twigs in glasses of water and watch them open.

Health: NAMES WILL NEVER HURT ME

Share the following rhyme with students.

> Sticks and stones may break my bones,
> But names will never hurt me.

Ask them if they think the last line of the poem is true. Invite students to suggest things they can do when others say things that hurt their feelings.

Game: NIM

Use twigs to play a game that originated in Denmark. To begin, break several sticks into sixteen 4-inch twigs. Place them on a flat surface in four columns (four twigs per column). Have students play in pairs, taking turns choosing from one to four twigs. The only rule is that the twigs chosen must be next to one another, either in adjoining rows or columns. The winner is the player who strategically sets up his or her opponent to take the last stick.

Language Arts: ABC TWIGS

Work with students to collect twigs that look like letters of the alphabet. See how many of the 26 letters they can find. Create the ones that are not found by tying separate twigs together with twine or string. Take a picture of each "twig letter" and create a twig alphabet book.

Literature Connections

The Three Little Pigs
by James Marshall (E.P. Dutton, 1989). In this version of the familiar tale, one of the pig brothers survives the wolf's attack by using his head and planning well.

A Tree Is Nice
by Janice May Udry (HarperCollins, 1956). This Caldecott award-winning classic shares the many reasons for appreciating trees. Students will enjoy adding their own ideas.

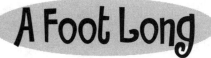

A Foot Long

Name _____ Date _____

Find objects that are longer than, shorter than, or the same as your stick.
Draw pictures of or write names for them here.

Longer Than ⟲	Shorter Than ⟲	The Same As

Investigating Snow & Ice

For young children, snow and ice seem to appear and disappear as if by magic. In this section, students investigate winter weather to learn its secrets. They'll investigate the shape of snowflakes, collect and record information about snowfall, estimate how many scoops of snow it takes to fill a bucket and see what happens when it melts, and more.

• **Related Themes: Winter, Weather, Matter**

Watch It Melt

Students observe, measure, and compare different amounts of snow before and after the melting process.

Skills and Concepts: fractions, volume

Steps

1 Fill three different-size containers one half, one third, and one quarter full of snow.

2 Make marks on the outside of the jars to indicate the levels of snow.

3 Ask students what will happen when the snow melts: *Will the jars still be one half, one third, and one quarter full?*

4 Let the snow melt and discuss the results.

Materials

- **three glass jars**
  (different sizes)
- **masking tape**
- **marker**
- **snow**

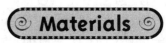

Snowflake Geometry

Materials

- **Snowflake Bentley** by Jacqueline Briggs Martin (Houghton Mifflin, 1998)
- **marshmallows** (regular and mini)
- **toothpicks**

Tip

The marshmallows will be easier to work with if you leave them unwrapped overnight.

Students discover that all snowflakes have six points.

Skills and Concepts: six-sided shapes

Steps

1 Share *Snowflake Bently*, then return to the page that shows the closeup of a snowflake. Explain that although no two snowflakes are alike, they all have six points. Demonstrate this concept by helping students create their own snowflakes.

2 Provide each student with one large marshmallow, six mini-marshmallows, and twelve toothpicks.

3 Instruct students to take the large marshmallow and hold it in a horizontal position. Guide them in spiraling six toothpicks (evenly spaced) around the marshmallow's middle.

4 Have students place one mini-marshmallow at the end of each toothpick. They can then connect each mini-marshmallow by using the six other toothpicks. Their finished "snowflake" should be in a hexagonal shape.

5 Ask students to look at their snowflakes and count the number of sides. Next, have them count the number of points. Explain that the shape they created is called a *hexagon* and that all hexagons have six sides and six points.

How Deep Is the Snow?

Take advantage of the weather outside by collecting, recording, and organizing snowfall data.

Skills and Concepts: measurement of depth, graphing

Steps

1 Insert the dowel into the ground in an open area away from buildings or trees. Label the dowel in one-inch increments.

2 Give each child a Snowfall Table record sheet. For a period of 20 days, take students outside on a daily basis to check the depth of the snow, using the dowel as a weather instrument. Have students record the date and depth of snow on their snowfall tables. For younger students, you may want to prepare a chart-size version of the table and fill it out as a class.

3 At the end of 20 days, work with students to create a graph based on the information they gathered. Ask students what information needs to be included in the graph (*date and number of inches*). Label the axes accordingly.

4 Display the graph and ask the following questions:

❀ Which day of the month had the most snow?

❀ Which had the least?

❀ How many more inches of snow did we have on _____(date) than on _____(date)?

Materials

- **wooden dowel** (approximately 4 feet long)
- **chart paper**
- **marker**
- **Snowfall Table** (see page 64)

Tip

If you live in an area that does not get snow, follow snowfall in another place using the newspaper weather map, or check the weather on the Internet at **www.accuweather.com**.

Snowfall Table

Name _____

Date _____

Date	Depth of Snow	Date	Depth of Snow

Bye, Bye Snowman

Students estimate and record the amount of time it takes for a snowman to melt.

Skills and Concepts: estimation of time, tallying, counting by ones and fives, numerical order

Steps

1 After a snowfall, go outside and build a snowman with students.

2 Discuss what will have to happen for the snowman to melt. (*The temperature needs to go above freezing, and so on.*)

3 Ask students to estimate how many days will go by before the snowman is completely melted. Have students record their estimates on the snowman patterns. Guide them in arranging their estimates in numerical order and taping them to a wall.

4 Keep track of the number of days by recording a tally mark on a snowman pattern for each day that the snowman is still standing. Count up the tally marks daily, demonstrating for students how to count by fives.

5 When the snowman is completely melted, add up the tally marks for a final count and compare students' estimates.

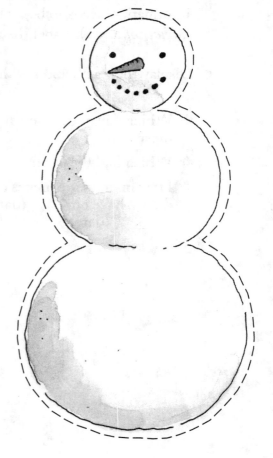

Materials

- **snowman accessories** (hat, scarf, and so on)
- **snowman pattern** (see below)
- **chart paper**
- **marker**
- **tape**
- **three glass jars** (different sizes)
- **masking tape**
- **marker**
- **snow**

Tip

Dress your snowman up for the birds by adding twig arms for perches. Add peanut butter-covered pinecone buttons, a popcorn garland belt, a raisin smile, and date eyes and nose.

How Many Scoops?

Bring snow indoors and challenge children to estimate the number of scoops it takes to fill different-size containers.

Skills and Concepts: estimation of volume, measurement of volume, counting by ones, numerical order

Steps

1 Have children cut out snowball shapes from white paper. (You may provide a four-inch circle as a template.)

2 Gather students in a circle. Show them one of the containers and ask how many cups of snow it will take to fill it. Invite them to record their estimates on the snowball shapes. Go around the cirlce and let students share their estimates.

3 Begin filling the container with snow. Count the cups aloud with students.

4 When the container is about half full, ask students if any of them want to change their estimates. Give them time to record a new estimate on their snowball patterns.

5 Go around the circle again and ask for new estimates. Encourage students to tell why they changed their estimates.

6 Continue scooping snow until the container is full. Ask students to tell whether their estimates were higher or lower than the actual amount.

7 Repeat the activity using different-sized containers.

Materials

- **white paper**
- **different-size containers**
- **snow** (use crushed ice or fake snow as a substitute)
- **one-cup measure**

Today's Temperature

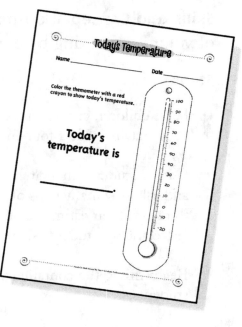

Materials

- **outdoor thermometer**
- **red crayon or marker**
- **Today's Temperature... record sheet** (see page 65)

Students become familiar with a thermometer and its freezing point as they practice reading and recording the temperature.

Skills and Concepts:
measuring temperature

Steps

1 Show students a thermometer. Point out its parts and discuss its purpose. Ask students if they know what temperature is the freezing point. (*32° Fahrenheit*)

2 Place a thermometer outside the classroom window (or in some other easily accessible location).

3 At the same time every day, read the thermometer with students. Model for students how to record the temperature on the record sheet.

4 Ask students if today's temperature is above or below the freezing point.

5 After several demonstrations, assign different pairs of students to record the temperature on a daily basis and share their findings with the class. Display the thermometer record sheet each day. Together, look for patterns over time.

6 To go further, graph the temperature each day. As students check the temperature, they can record it on the thermometer record sheet and on the graph. Look for patterns on the graph.

Extra, Extra...

Literature Connections

Science and Nature: THE GREAT MELTDOWN

Give groups of students an ice cube, a cafeteria tray, salt, black construction paper, a foam cup, and aluminum foil. Challenge each group to be the first one to melt the ice cube. Encourage students to use the materials they were given or anything else in the room they think will help speed up the process. After the ice cubes have melted, ask group members to explain how they accomplished their task.

Art: NATURE COLLAGES

Give each student a disposable pie tin filled with water. Invite children to place natural objects in their tin. Place the ends of a loop of yarn in the water, then place the tins outside and let them freeze solid. Once frozen, pour some warm water on the back of the pie tins to unmold the ice. Hang the ice from a tree or fence outside the classroom window for students to enjoy.

Language Arts: SNOWMAN TALK

Share the following poem with students.

HOW TO TALK TO YOUR SNOWMAN

Use words that are pleasing,
Like: freezing
And snow,
Iceberg and igloo
And blizzard and blow,
Try: Arctic, Antarctic,
Say: shiver and shake,
But whatever you say,
Never say: bake.

—*Beverly McLoughland*

Ask students what many of the words in the poem have in common. Ask students to list "cold" and "hot" words on a chart. Using the chart as a reference, have students write their own poems by completing the poetry pattern on page 66. Put students' pages together to make a class book.

Sadie and the Snowman

by Allen Morgan (Kids Can Press, 1985). Kids will delight in Sadie's creative attempts to protect her snowman from rising temperatures and animals that eat his cracker eyes, carrot nose, and zucchini smile.

Snowballs

by Lois Ehlert (Harcourt Brace, 1995). After collecting lots and lots of "stuff" like seeds, nuts, and yarn, children create a snow family. The book includes photos of snowmen, information about how snow is formed, and a recipe for popcorn balls.

Snow is Falling

by Franklyn M. Branley (HarperCollins, 1986). Simple nonfiction text reveals the properties of snow and how it can be good for plants, animals, and people.

Snowfall Table

Name _____ Date _____

Date	Depth of Snow	Date	Depth of Snow

Hands-On Math Around the Year • Scholastic Professional Books

Name _____ Date _____

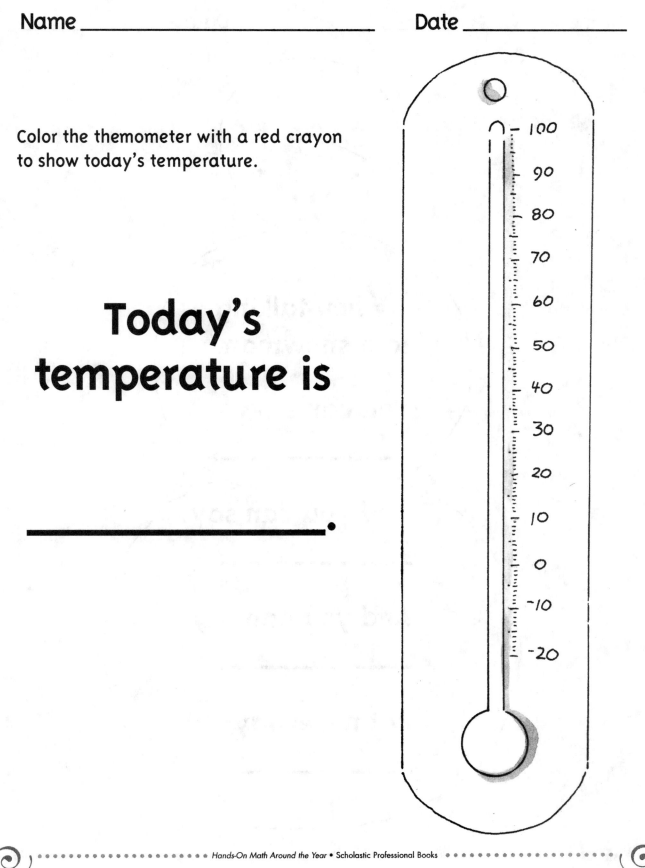

Color the themometer with a red crayon
to show today's temperature.

Today's
temperature is

_____ .

Name _____   Date _____

When talking
to a snowman,

You can say

_____,

And you can say

_____,

And you can say

_____,

But never say

_____!

Finding Out About Feathers

What is as light as a feather? How many different ways can feathers be sorted? Do bird feathers have patterns? In this section, students discover the answers to these and other questions as they experiment with weight, make Venn diagrams, continue patterns, learn about place value, and more.

● **Related Themes: Birds**

Our Fine-Feathered Friends

Students examine patterns in bird feathers and create patterns of their own.

Skills and Concepts: patterns

Steps

1 Show students some real feathers or pictures of birds. Ask them to describe the patterns they see in the feathers.

2 Give students feather patterns and crayons or markers. Have them create their own patterns on the feathers.

3 Cut out a large bird (without feathers) from construction paper and staple it to a bulletin board. Let students place their completed feathers on the bird.

Materials

- **real feathers or close-up pictures of birds**
- **feather pattern** (see page 73)
- **crayons or markers**
- **construction paper**
- **scissors**
- **stapler**

As Light as a Feather

◎ Materials ◎

- **one feather**
- **balance scale**

⊙Tip

For most of the activities in this section, synthetic feathers will be suitable. They are available in most craft stores or can be ordered from Oriental Trading Company, Inc., P.O. Box 2308, Omaha, NE 68103-2308; (800) 228-2269; **www.oriental.com**. However, you will still need a few real feathers for some of the activities. Depending on where you live, you may look for feathers on the ground, at the shore, near a pond, or at a farm. When using real feathers, wash them first. Some birds are known to carry disease.

Students explore a common expression to learn about weight.

Skills and Concepts: measuring weight

Steps

1 Gather students in a circle. Pass around a feather and let them feel how light it is. Ask: *What do you think the expression "As light as a feather" means?* (See page 72 for a related language arts activity on similes.)

2 Challenge each student to find an object in the classroom that is "as light as a feather." Have children bring their objects back to the circle.

3 Place the balance scale in the center of the circle. One at a time, let students test their object to see if it is "as light as a feather." Sort the objects into two piles—those that are "as light as a feather" and those that are not.

4 Let students conduct further investigation on their own to find more objects that are "as light as a feather." Have them make record sheets (see sample, right) and use pictures to show what they find.

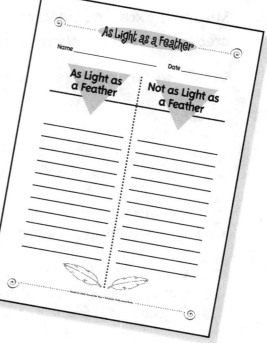

Making Venn Diagrams

While sorting and classifying feathers, students explore Venn diagrams as a tool for organizing information.

Skills and Concepts: sorting and classifying, using Venn diagrams

Steps

1 Sort the feathers into groups by color. Ask students to guess your sorting rule. Write the name of each color group (for example, "red," "yellow," and so on) on an index card.

2 Continue sorting the feathers other ways—for example, real/not real, patterned/not patterned, small/medium/large, and so on. Let students guess each sorting rule. Write each part of the sorting rule on an index card—for example, "Real" on one card, "Not Real" on another.

3 Create a Venn diagram (two overlapping circles) using string or two hula hoops. Choose two index card labels from step 2 (from different sorting rules) and place one in each circle. So, you might place the label "Real" in one circle and the label "Small" in the other circle.

4 Hold up a feather and demonstrate how to decide where it goes in the Venn diagram. Tell students that feathers that fall into both categories go in the overlapping part of the two circles, and feathers that don't fit into any of the categories are set outside of the circles. Place the feather in the appropriate spot.

5 Ask a student to choose a second feather, explain where it goes in the Venn diagram, and place it in the appropriate spot. Continue this process until all feathers have been sorted.

6 Choose two more index cards and repeat the activity. Place the feathers at a center and let children experiment with sorting the feathers on their own.

Materials

- **synthetic feathers** (five to ten)
- **real feathers** (five to ten)
- **index cards**
- **marker**
- **string or two hula hoops**

Place-Value Plumage

Students apply their knowledge of place value by representing two-digit numbers with birds and feathers.

Skills and Concepts: place value

Materials

- **index cards**
- **marker**
- **craft feathers**
- **bird patterns**
  (see page 73)

Steps

1 Write two-digit numbers on index cards and place them at a center with a bag of feathers and several bird patterns. (You may want to laminate the patterns for durability.)

2 Model how to represent one of the numbers using the feathers and bird patterns. For example, if you select the number *23*, place ten feathers on each of two bird patterns. Leave three feathers loose on the table.

3 Let students visit the center independently or with a partner to use the materials. Encourage them to show you or a partner their work.

4 For additional practice, call out numbers and ask students to come up to the chalkboard and represent the number with drawings of birds and feathers.

Two Birds of a Feather

Students manipulate birds and feathers to represent addition facts and number combinations.

Skills and Concepts: addition, number combinations

Steps

1 Display two bird patterns. Place feathers on each bird—for example, four on one and three on the other. Ask students: *How many feathers are on each bird? How many feathers are there all together?* Write their answers as a number sentence: 4 + 3 = 7. Repeat the activity with two different numbers. Invite a student to write the number sentence represented by the feathers on the board.

2 Give each student two bird patterns and 10 to 12 feathers. Write a number sentence on the board. Ask students to show that number sentence using their feathers and birds. Repeat this with several other number sentences.

3 Ask each student to take five feathers and divide them up between the two birds any way they choose. Have students glue their birds to a sheet of construction paper and write the number sentence that goes with their birds.

4 Let students take turns sharing their birds and number sentences. Write the different ways of making 5 on the chalkboard.

5 Repeat steps 3 and 4 using different numbers. Let children continue on their own, using their feathers to make new number sentences.

Materials

- **bird patterns** (see page 73)
- **feathers** (10–12 per student)
- **construction paper**

Tip

Find out about real birds! *First Field Guides: Birds* (Scholastic, 1998) contains facts, photographs, and illustrations for more than 150 birds, including 50 that are likely to be found in North America. A water-resistant "spotter's card" makes it easy to identify birds in the field.

Literature Connections

Feathers for Lunch
by Lois Ehlert (Voyager Picture Books, 1996). Children will enjoy the sneaky cat that tries to catch tasty birds for lunch and will learn how to identify twelve common birds.

The Secret of the Eagle Feathers
by Maura Elizabeth Keleher McKinley (Raintree/Steck Vaughn, 1997). An Indian girl, with the help of an eagle and a coyote, finds her grandfather's stolen headdress and learns the secret that made him a great leader.

Yettele's Feathers
by Joan Rothenberg (Hyperion Books, 1995). Yettele, who loves to gossip, shrugs off her neighbors' complaints by telling them her stories are only words and words are no more hurtful than feathers.

Extra, Extra...

Art: FEATHER PENS
Students may find it hard to believe, but 200 years ago quill pens were the most popular way to write. Let students use feathers to simulate quill pens of the past. Have them snip the end to make a point, then dip the feathers in paint or India ink to write.

Science: WATER-RESISTANT FEATHERS
When birds preen their feathers, they use a waxy oil that comes from a gland at the base of their tail. This oil helps to waterproof their feathers. In addition, birds' feathers have *barbs* (hooked bristles) that stick together and keep the water out. Provide small groups of students with a feather and an eyedropper full of water. Have them drop water on the feather and describe what happens.

Music and Movement: FIVE LITTLE DUCKS
Share the song "Five Little Ducks" with students. (See page 74.) Let them take turns being the five little ducks and acting out the song. Give one student a feather and let him or her be the "one little duck with the feather on his back."

Language Arts: AS LIGHT AS A FEATHER
Write the expression "as light as a feather" on a piece of chart paper. Explain that this is called a *simile*. A simile compares two things using the words *like* or *as*. Follow up by sharing *Quick as a Cricket* by Audrey Wood (Child's Play, 1990). Give each student a piece of paper with either of the following simile frames written on it: _____ *as* _____ or _____ *like* _____ .
Ask students to create their own similes and draw pictures to go with them. Compile the work into a book.

72

Feather Pattern

Name _____ Date _____

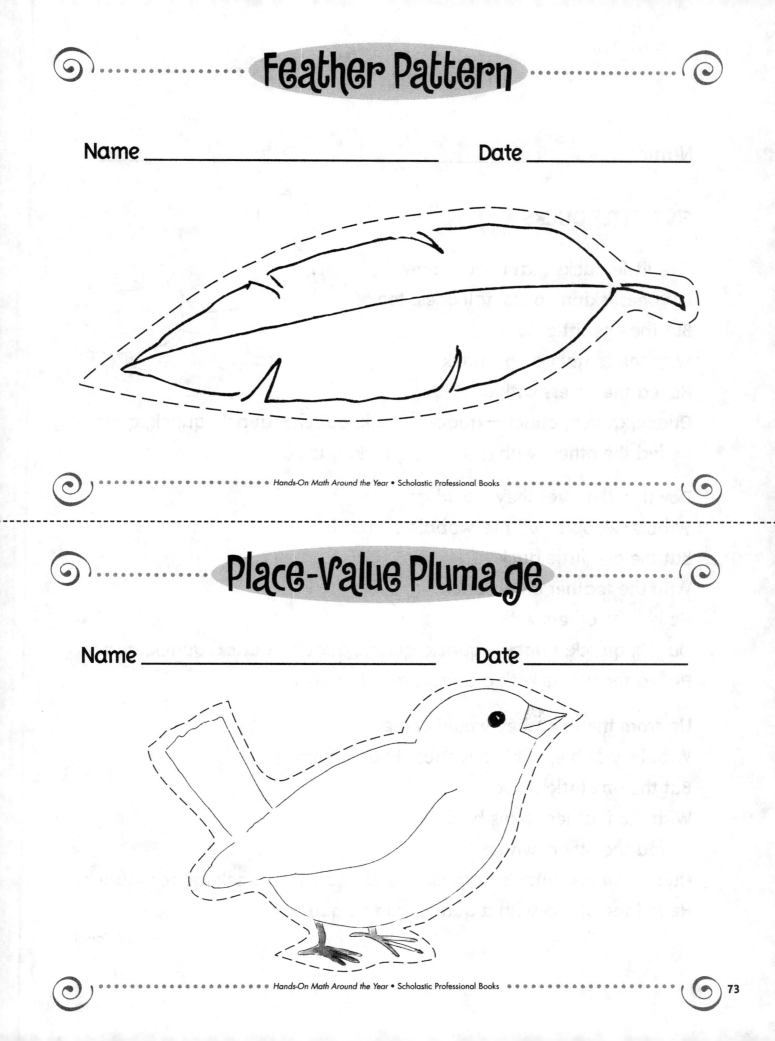

Place-Value Plumage

Name _____ Date _____

Five Little Ducks

Name _____   **Date** _____

FIVE LITTLE DUCKS

Five little ducks that I once knew
Fat ones, skinny ones, tall ones, too.
But the one little duck
With the feather on his back
He led the others with a
Quack, quack, quack – quack, quack, quack – quack, quack, quack
He led the others with a quack, quack, quack.

Down to the river they would go
Wibble-wobble, wibble-wobble to and fro.
But the one little duck
With the feather on his back
He led the others with a
Quack, quack, quack – quack, quack, quack – quack, quack, quack
He led the others with a quack, quack, quack.

Up from the river they would come
Wibble-wobble, wibble-wobble to and fro
But the one little duck
With the feather on his back
He led the others with a
Quack, quack, quack – quack, quack, quack – quack, quack, quack
He led the others with a quack, quack, quack.

– Traditional

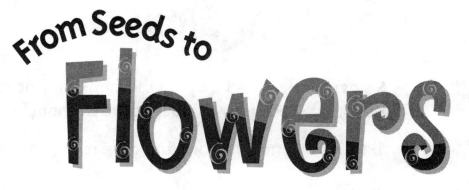

From Seeds to Flowers

Every flower begins as a seed—and that's where your students will begin with the activities in this section. They'll examine a wide assortment of seeds and find different ways to sort them. As gardening consumers, they'll "purchase" seeds and practice counting change. When it's time to plant, they'll track and graph growth.

- **Related Themes: Plants, Spring**

Seed Sort

Students examine and sort seeds using a graphic organizer.

Skills and Concepts: sorting and classifying

Steps

1 Give each student a Seed Sorting Mat and some seeds.

2 Ask students to dump the seeds into the center circle on their sorting mats and sort them (in any way) into the smaller circles. Let students know that they do not have to use all of the circles. Have students glue the seeds in place and write about their sorting rules.

3 Invite students to share their sorting mats with the class and tell how they sorted their seeds. Record their ideas on chart paper. As a follow-up, have children place their sorting mats between sheets of clear contact paper. They make great reusable place mats!

Materials

- **Seed Sorting Mat** (see page 81)
- **assorted seeds**
- **paper cups or resealable bags** (one per student)
- **glue**
- **chart paper**
- **marker**

Garden Shop

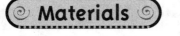

Materials

- **assorted flower seeds**
- **small, shallow containers** (such as yogurt-cup lids)
- **magnetic coins** (real coins with magnetic tape attached to the back)
- **magnetic surface** (such as a cookie sheet)
- **sandwich bags** (six per student)

Students select and display the coins they need to purchase seeds from a class "garden shop."

Skills and Concepts: counting change

Steps

1 Set up a garden shop in your classroom. On a table or counter, display containers of different flower seeds. Make small signs that tell the seed type and price. Place signs next to the seeds.

2 Each morning, gather students together and let several students choose six seeds to purchase from the garden shop.

3 Guide students in manipulating the coins on the magnetic surface to display how much they need to purchase the seeds. Count the coins aloud with the class to practice counting change.

4 Place the seeds in sandwich bags and label with the names of the seeds and students' names. Save for use with "How Does My Garden Grow?" (page 82).

How Does My Garden Grow?

Students plant seeds and watch them grow, recording changes over time.

Skills and Concepts:

measuring, graphing, time

Steps

1 Have students assign their Garden Shop seeds numbers from 1 to 6.

2 Give each child half an egg carton with lid intact. Have children label the lids to show the name, number, and position of the seeds they will plant.

3 Assist students in planting the seeds by filling the egg carton cups with soil and placing each seed in the corresponding numbered cup. Have students place their egg cartons in a sunny spot. Remind them to add water when the soil is dry.

4 Show students how to keep track of how much time passes until the seeds sprout by coloring in a square for each seed to represent each passing day. When a seed sprouts, students can stop coloring in squares for that particular seed.

5 After a 20-day period, guide students in discussing results. Be sure to compare results among students.

❀ How many seeds sprouted?
❀ How many seeds didn't sprout?
❀ Which seed sprouted first?
❀ How many days did it take for the first seed to sprout?
❀ Which seed sprouted last?
❀ How many days did it take for the last seed to sprout?

Materials

- **seeds** (see Garden Shop, page 76)
- **How Does My Garden Grow? record sheet** (see page 82)
- **egg cartons cut in half** (one half for each student)
- **soil**
- **crayons**

Tip

Find out more about flowers! *First Field Guides: Flowers* (Scholastic, 1998) contains facts, photographs, and illustrations for more than 150 flowers, including 50 that are likely to be found in North America. A water-resistant "spotter's card" makes it easy to identify flowers in the field.

From Little Sprout to Green Giant

Materials

- **plastic cups**
  (one per student)
- **soil**
- **marigold seeds**
- **water**
- **tongue depressors**
  (one per student)
- **rulers**
  (one per student)
- **pencils**
- **My Plant Journal record sheets**
  (see page 83)
- **paper**
- **crayons**
- **stapler**

Students make plant rulers and use them to journal the growth of a seed.

Skills and Concepts: measurement of length, recording data

Steps

1 Provide each student with a plastic cup, some soil, and some marigold seeds. Have students fill their cups about two-thirds with soil, then place the seeds on top, sprinkle with soil to cover, and add water to moisten.

2 Have students place the cups near a window. Remind them to water the plants to keep the soil moist.

3 Before the seeds sprout, make tools for measuring growth. Give each child a tongue depressor, ruler, and pencil. Guide students in following these steps:

- ✿ Measure the tongue depressor. Draw a line across the tongue depressor at the one-inch mark.

- ✿ Match up the edge of the ruler with the line on the tongue depressor. Draw additional lines in half-inch increments. Label them from one to four inches.

- ✿ Insert the stick into the soil, stopping at the first line.

4 Give each child multiple copies of "My Plant Journal." (See page 00.) Provide a copy for each day you want students to observe their plants. Let students illustrate a cover and staple the journal pages together.

5 Have students use words and pictures to record observations of their plants, including changes in height.

Flower Garden Glyphs

Students create flower glyphs to display and present information about themselves.

Skills and Concepts: organizing and representing information, measuring length, counting by ones

Steps

1 Explain that long ago people told stories by carving pictures, called *glyphs*, into cave walls. Copy the legend (see below) on posterboard or the chalkboard. Use the legend to make a flower glyph that tells about you. Invite students to take turns telling what information they can gather from the glyph.

2 Give students construction paper, scissors, glue, pencils, and seeds. Have them use the materials to make glyphs that tell about them.

3 Display flower glyphs around the classroom. Each day select a couple of glyphs and have classmates try to determine who they describe.

LEGEND

CENTER OF FLOWER	Brown = I have brown hair. Black = I have black hair. Red = I have red hair. Yellow = I have yellow hair.
PETALS	One petal for each letter in your first name
SEEDS	One seed for each person in your family
STEM	One inch of stem for each foot of your height
LEAVES	One leaf = I am a boy. Two leaves = I am a girl.

Materials

- **construction paper** (including brown, red, black, yellow, and green)
- **scissors**
- **glue**
- **pencils**
- **seeds** (any kind)

Alison's Zinnia

by Anita Lobel (Greenwillow, 1990). Alison acquired an amaryllis for Beryl, who bought a begonia for Crystal, and so begins this interlocking alphabet book that's not only fun, but visually appealing.

Flower Garden

by Eve Bunting (Harcourt Brace, 1994). Told in a simple rhyme, a little girl and her father prepare a flower garden as a birthday surprise for her mother.

I'm a Seed

by Jean Marzollo (Cartwheel Books, 1996). A pumpkin seed and a marigold seed grow side by side and discuss the changes they are going through.

The Tiny Seed

by Eric Carle (Picture Book Studios, 1987). With collage illustrations and simple text, this book follows the life cycle of a flower through the seasons.

Extra, Extra...

Language Arts: SEED HOUSES

Read *A House is a House for Me* by Mary Ann Hoberman (Viking, 1978). Follow up by showing students an apple. Ask: *What is this a house for?* (an apple seed) Do the same with other fruits. Try a pinecone, too. Create a class book by having students complete the following sentence frame: *A _____ is a house for a _____ seed.* Let students illustrate their sentences. Staple the pages together with a cover to make a book.

Snack: GOOD ENOUGH TO EAT

Give each student one round cracker, six apple slices, one tablespoon of peanut butter, six raisins, and one pretzel stick. Follow these steps to create edible flowers.

- Spread peanut butter on the cracker. Top with raisins.
- Arrange the apple slices around the cracker to form petals.
- Add a pretzel stick stem.

Safety Tip: *Be sure to check on allergies before serving any food.*

Music and Movement: LITTLE CRADLES

Share the following poem with students. (See page 84.)

LITTLE CRADLES

In their little cradles,
Packed in tight,
Baby seeds are sleeping,
Out of sight.
Mr. Wind comes blowing,
With all his might,
The baby seeds are scattered,
Left and right.

—Author Unknown

Invite students to become the seeds by squatting down and wrapping their arms around their legs. Let one child weave in and out of the "sleeping seeds," making wind noises. At the end of the poem, students can pop up and scatter around the classroom.

Seed Sorting Mat

Name _____ Date _____

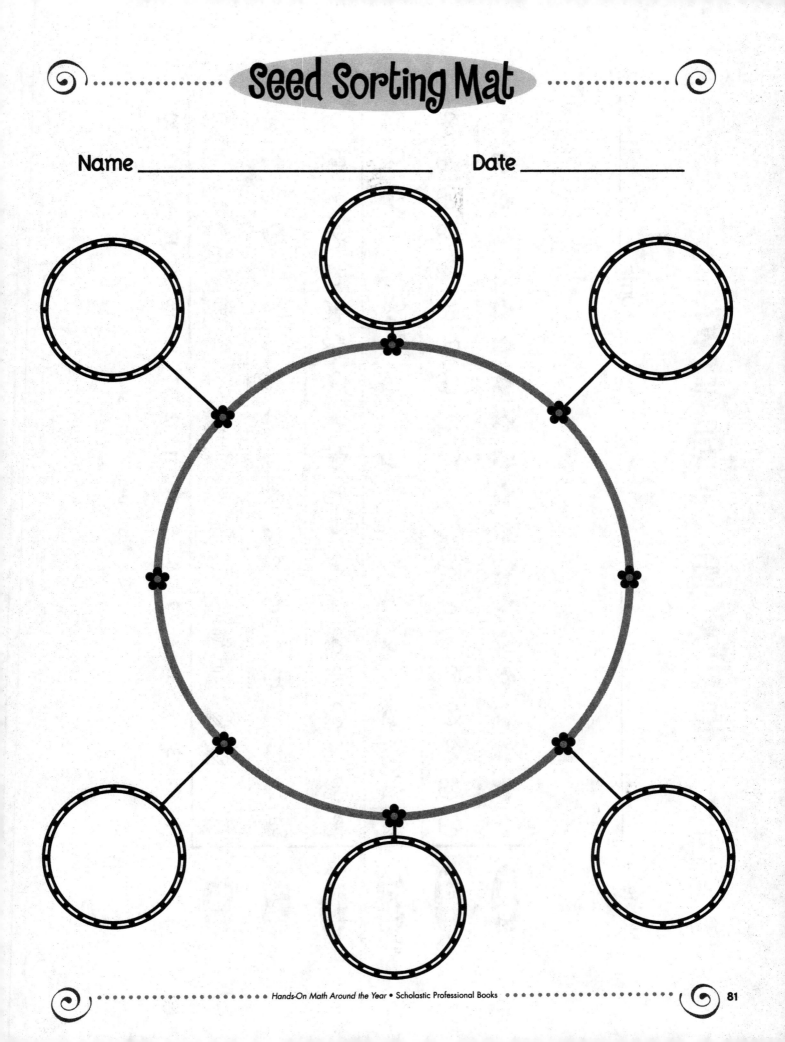

How Does My Garden Grow?

Name _____

Date _____

	seed 1	seed 2	seed 3	seed 4	seed 5	seed 6

Number of Days

1 2 3 4 5 6 7 8 9 10 11 12 13 14 15 16 17 18 19 20

Hands-On Math Around the Year • Scholastic Professional Books

My Plant Journal

Name _____

I observed my plant on

_____.
(date)

My plant is _____ high:

My observations in a picture:

My Plant Journal

Name _____

I observed my plant on

_____.
(date)

My plant is _____ high:

My observations in a picture:

Name _____   Date _____

LITTLE CRADLES

In their little cradles,
Packed in tight,
Baby seeds are sleeping,
Out of sight.
Mr. Wind comes blowing,
With all his might,
The baby seeds are scattered,
Left and right.

—Author Unknown

Try This!

- Share the poem with your family. Let one person read the poem aloud.
  Take turns being the seeds and the wind. Show how you move!

I Spy Shells

There's something magical about shells. Children love looking at and collecting these gifts from nature. They'll quickly be drawn into activities that use shells, such as counting, adding, and subtracting. There are also patterns to extend and create, an attribute-matching activity, and a shell game to play.

- **Related Themes: Oceans, Sea Life, Seashore**

Shells on the Beach

Students count out shells to match number words or numerals written on sandpaper beaches.

Skills and Concepts: number word recognition, numeral recognition, counting by ones

Steps

1 Make ten copies of the story mat. Label them 1 to 10.

2 Place the story mats at a center with a bucket of 55 shells.

3 Invite students to place the correct number of seashells on each story mat beach.

Materials

- **Beach Story Mat** (see page 91)
- **scissors**
- **marker**
- **bucket**
- **55 shells**

Seashell Stories

Materials

- **Beach Story Mat** (see page 91)
- **shells** (10–12 per student)

Tip

If you aren't in a location where you can easily collect shells from a beach, you can purchase shells from Teacher Resource Center (800) 833-3389. You can also make copies of the shells on page 90.

Students manipulate shells on sandpaper beaches as they listen to story problems.

Skills and Concepts: addition, subtraction, recording number sentences

Steps

1 Give each student a story mat and some shells. (Students can use the materials from this activity with the poem "Five Little Seashells" on page 92.)

2 Call out an addition or subtraction story problem. Assist students in manipulating the shells to represent the story problems.

3 Have students record the number sentences—for example, $4 + 3 = 7$— that correspond to the story problems.

4 Invite students to write or tell their own story problems to share with the class.

Seashell Patterns

Students read, copy, and extend shell patterns.

Skills and Concepts: reading, copying, and extending patterns

- **assorted shells**
- **card stock strips** (approximately 12 inches long each)
- **glue gun** (for teacher use only)

Steps

1 Glue shells on strips of card stock to form different patterns.

2 Choose one of the pattern strips and demonstrate for students one way to read the pattern—for example, *big, little, little, big, little, little,* and so on.

3 If possible, demonstrate a different way to read the same pattern—for example, *striped, striped, plain, striped, striped, plain,* and so on. Continue naming different ways to read the same pattern while eliciting ideas from students.

4 Choose a different pattern strip and repeat steps 1 to 3.

5 Place pattern strips and shells at a center and invite students to copy and extend the patterns. (They can use the shells to extend the patterns or draw pictures of the shells on blank strips of paper.)

The Shell Game

In this game, students rely on problem-solving abilities to determine how many shells are under a bowl.

Skills and Concepts: problem solving, number combinations, addition, subtraction

Materials

- **bowls**
  (one for every two students)
- **shells**

Steps

1 Give pairs of students a bowl and some shells. Determine the number of shells by selecting a number you want children to explore—for example, *8*. (Children will then work to make combinations that equal 8, such as $4+4$, $2+6$, $3+5$, $0+8$.)

2 Have one partner place some of the shells under the bowl and the rest on top. Have the other partner tell how many shells are under the bowl. Repeat to provide plenty of chances to play.

3 Have students record the combinations they come up with, either by recording number sentences or by drawing shells.

Shell Hunt

Students use spatial sense and attributes to match outlines to shells.

Skills and Concepts: spatial relationships, attributes

Materials

- **shells**
  (one per student)
- **paper**
- **plastic dish tub**
- **play sand**

Steps

1 Give each student a seashell and a piece of paper. Assist students in tracing around their shells to produce an outline.

2 Bury some of the shells in a tub of play sand and place the tub and corresponding outlines at a center. Invite students to dig for shells and match them to the outlines. Rotate the shells and outline so that every student's shell is included.

Extra, Extra...

Science and Nature: MAKING FOSSILS

Give each student a shell. Assist students in coating the shells with petroleum jelly. Instruct them to press their shells halfway into a cupcake liner filled with wet plaster. When the plaster hardens, students can slide their seashells out to see their fossils!

Science and Nature: SHELL RESEARCH

Give small groups of students a shell. Provide them with books about seashells. Challenge them to find out what type of animal lived in that shell. Invite each group to share its findings with the class.

Music and Movement: FIVE LITTLE SEASHELLS

Share the following rhyme with students. Let students act out the rhyme. Five can be "shells" and the rest can be "waves," with the shells disappearing one by one and the waves going "swish." Give students copies of the poem (see page 92) and invite them to act it out with their families.

FIVE LITTLE SEASHELLS

Five little seashells washed up on the shore,
Along came a wave and then there were four.
Four little seashells happy as could be,
Along came a wave and then there were three.
Three little seashells all shiny new,
Along came a wave and then there were two.
Two little seashells lying in the sun,
Along came a wave and then there was one.
One little seashell left all alone,
Put it in your pocket and take it home.

—Author Unknown

A House for Hermit Crab

by Eric Carle (Picture Book Studio, 1987). When the hermit crab outgrows his shell, he decides to search for a new one.

Is This a House for Hermit Crab?

by Megan McDonald (Orchard Books, 1990). Hermit crab needs a new home. He tries a rock, an old tin can, a piece of driftwood, and other objects. But nothing suits his needs. Will he ever find the right home?

What Lives in a Shell?

by Kathleen Weidner Zoehfeld (HarperCollins, 1994). This simple non-fiction book illustrates the many different animals that make their homes inside shells.

What's Inside Shells?

by Angela Royston (Dorling Kindersley, 1991). Real photographs with drawings show the wonders and workings of life inside shells.

Seashell Patterns

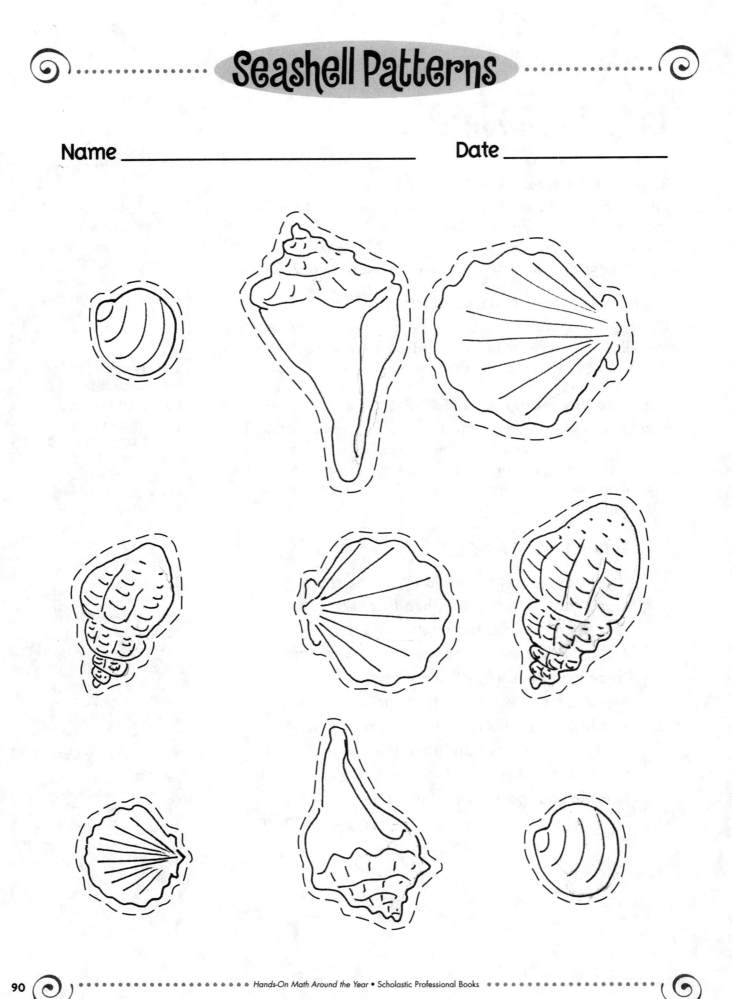

Hands-On Math Around the Year • Scholastic Professional Books

Beach Story Mat

Name _____   Date _____

Name _____   Date _____

FIVE LITTLE SEASHELLS

Five little seashells washed up on the shore,
Along came a wave and then there were four.
Four little seashells happy as could be,
Along came a wave and then there were three.
Three little seashells all shiny new,
Along came a wave and then there were two.
Two little seashells lying in the sun,
Along came a wave and then there was one.
One little seashell left all alone,
Put it in your pocket and take it home.

— Author Unknown

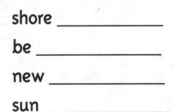

Try This!

• Find the rhyming word pairs in the poem.
  We found the first word in each pair for you.

    shore _____

    be _____

    new _____

    sun _____

• Find the number words in the poem. Write them here.

_____ _____ _____ _____ _____

• How many times can you find the word *seashells*? _____

Rounding Up Rocks

Children seem to be as drawn to rocks as they are to shells. Sometimes the rocks are smooth and feel good to hold. Other times the rocks have shiny particles and look like gems. In this section, students will use favorite rocks to learn about liquid measurement. They'll also explore weight, play sorting and attribute games, and work with number combinations.

● **Related Themes: Earth**

The Attribute Game

Challenge your students' classifying skills with an activity that looks at how objects are alike and different.

Skills and Concepts: sorting and classifying

Steps

1 Gather 20 to 30 small objects (including one rock) and place them in a pile. Have students sit in a circle around the objects.

2 Take the rock from the pile and set it in front of you. Ask students if they can find another object in the pile that has one attribute in common with the rock—for example, same color, size, shape, texture, use. Choose one student to select one such object and place it next to the rock.

3 Repeat step 2 using the object that the student chose. Continue this process until there are no objects left in the pile that share any of the attributes of the last object chosen. For a greater challenge, play the game again and find objects that share two attributes.

● **Materials**

● **20-30 rocks** (assorted types and sizes)

Rising Waters

Students experiment with the effects of rock size and number on water levels.

Skills and Concepts: liquid measurement

Steps

Materials

- **old shower curtain**
- **one plastic transparent container** (32 ounces or larger)
- **water**
- **measuring cup**
- **blue food-coloring**
- **masking tape or permanent marker**
- **15-20 rocks of different sizes and shapes**

Tip

Challenge children to round up a few rocks each and in no time you'll have a classroom quarry to use with the activities in this section. Check hobby stores for a few out-of-the-ordinary specimens.

1 Place the shower curtain on the floor. Gather students around it. (Or do this activity outdoors.) Fill the plastic container with two cups of water. Add blue food-coloring to make it more visible. Mark the two-cup level with tape or a permanent marker.

2 Ask students what will happen if a rock is added to the water. Will the water level remain the same? Drop a rock in the water to test their predictions. Continue dropping different-size rocks into the water to see how they affect the water level.

3 Remove the rocks from the container. Add two more cups of water to the container and mark the four-cup level. Take out two cups of water so that two remain in the container.

4 Ask students how many rocks they think it will take to bring the water level up from two cups to four cups. Go around the circle and have them share their predictions.

5 Begin dropping rocks into the container, one at a time, until the water level moves from two to four cups. Remove the rocks and count them. Compare with students' predictions. Repeat step 6 using different rocks. Did the number of rocks needed to go from two to four cups change? Why?

6 Place several rocks and the container filled with two cups of water at a center. Allow students to experiment adding rocks to raise the water level to four cups. Challenge them to determine where they think the three-cup mark would be. Let them experiment with adding rocks to bring the water level to this mark.

Greater Than, Less Than, Equal To

Students sort rocks by estimated weight, then measure them to check their guesses.

Skills and Concepts: measurement of weight; concept of *greater than, less than, equal to*; graphing; sorting and classifying

Steps

1 Place ten rocks, the balance scale, copies of the record sheet, and a crayon at a center.

2 Invite students to visit the center, choose one rock, and trace its shape in the space provided on the record sheet.

3 Students should then measure the weight of the rock using the balance scale and gram weights. If gram weights are unavailable, nonstandard units may be substituted. Have students record the weight on the record sheet.

4 Have students sort the other nine rocks into piles representing rocks they think are greater than, less than, and equal to the weight of the first rock.

5 Have students test their predictions by measuring each rock against the first, then record results by completing the graph on the record sheet.

6 Once all students have had a chance to visit the center, gather them together with their record sheets. Ask students to share with you the weight of the rock they chose. Ask individual students the following questions:

✿ How many rocks had a weight greater than your rock?
✿ How many rocks had a weight equal to your rock?
✿ How many rocks had a weight less than your rock?

Materials

- **ten rocks** (different sizes and shapes)
- **balance scale**
- **Greater Than, Less Than, Equal To record sheet** (see page 100)
- **crayons**
- **gram weights or non-standard measuring units** (such as blocks, cubes, or tiles)
- **marker**

Guess My Sorting Rule

Students explore characteristics of rocks and use attributes to sort them.

Skills and Concepts: sorting by attribute

Steps

1 Divide the rocks into five groups by the following sets of attributes: shiny-dull, smooth-rough, big-little, long-short, and light-dark. Use paper plates to separate one attribute in each set from the other.

2 Place each sorted group of rocks at a different location in your classroom and number them 1 to 5.

3 Divide students into five teams. Assign each team a set of rocks. Ask students to work together to guess the sorting rule. Have each team record the number of the set of rocks and the sorting rule on a sheet of paper. Rotate teams until each has visited each set of rocks.

4 Gather students in a circle. Display rock set number 1. Ask students from each team to share the way they think the rocks were sorted. If answers differ, have teams explain their thinking. Explore the possibility that there may be more than one way to label each sorted group. Continue displaying and discussing groups 2 to 5.

Materials

- **50–60 assorted rocks**
- **ten paper plates**
- **paper**
- **pencils**

Tip

Further explore characteristics of rocks with an "I Spy" game. Gather students in a circle. Place several rocks in the center. Choose one rock and have students ask you "yes or no" questions about it. Challenge them to try and guess the rock before they've asked ten questions.

The Hardness Test

Students sort rocks after performing a simple hardness test.

Skills and Concepts: sorting and classifying, graphing

Steps

1 Tell students that scientists sometimes test rocks for hardness to help them identify different types of rocks. Give each student six rocks, a penny, a fork, and four sheets of paper. Have students label their papers "Soft," "Medium-Hard," "Harder," and "Hardest."

2 Have students follow this process to test the hardness of their rocks:

✿ Scratch each rock with a fingernail. If the scratch leaves a mark, place the rock on the sheet labeled "Soft."

✿ Test the remaining rocks using the penny. If it scratches any of these rocks, place them on the sheet labeled "Medium-Hard."

✿ Test the remaining rocks using the fork. If it leaves a mark on any of these rocks, place them on the sheet labeled "Harder."

✿ If there are any rocks left at this point, place them on the sheet labeled "Hardest."

3 Have students record results using the Hardness Test circle graph. For each Soft rock, students color one piece of the circle red; Medium-Hard, blue; Harder, yellow; Hardest, green. Be sure to tell students that all of the pieces in the same color should be next to each other on the graph. Have students color in the key to show what each color represents.

4 Display and discuss the graphs:

✿ What information do the graphs tell you?

✿ Is there a way to tell how many of each type of rock there are?

✿ Can we tell just by looking (or do we have to count) which type of rock we have the most of? Least of?

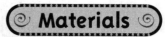

Materials

- **rocks** (six per student)
- **pennies** (one per student)
- **stainless steel forks** (one per student)
- **paper** (four sheets per student)
- **crayons**
- **Hardness Test graph** (see page 101)

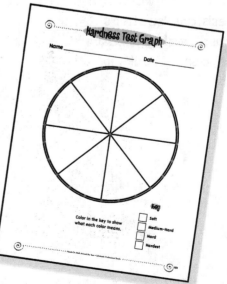

Pebbles in My Pockets

This game invites children to explore different ways to say the same number.

Skills and Concepts: addition, subtraction, number combinations

Steps

1 Decide which number combinations you want to work on— for example, combinations that equal 5—and place that many pebbles in the pockets of the jacket (some in one pocket, the rest in the other). Put on the jacket.

2 Tell students the total number of pebbles you have in your pockets. Ask them to guess how many are in your right pocket and how many are in your left.

3 Write students' guesses on the chalkboard to remind them of the combinations they have already guessed.

4 Let the student who guesses correctly wear the jacket and decide how many pebbles go in each pocket. (If necessary, guide students who need support so that everyone gets a chance to wear the jacket.) Continue, using the same number of pebbles or changing the number to reinforce combinations for different numbers.

Materials

- **a jacket with two pockets**
- **10–12 pebbles**

Tip

Find out more about using attributes to identify rocks. First *Field Guides: Rocks and Minerals* (Scholastic, 1998) contains facts, photographs, and illustrations for more than 175 rocks and minerals. A water-resistant "spotter's card" makes it easy to identify rocks in the field.

Extra, Extra...

Snack: EDIBLE ROCKS

Tell students that rocks are made up of minerals. Illustrate this concept by helping them create their own edible rocks. Melt 40 marshmallows and 3 tablespoons of butter in a large pan. Stir in 6 cups of puffed rice cereal. Drop spoonfuls of the mixture onto waxed paper for each student. Let it cool a little so students can handle it without burning themselves. Provide them with "minerals" (raisins, nuts, and chocolate chips) and let students add them to their "rocks." Once their rocks are formed, they can eat them.

Safety Tip: *Be sure to check on allergies before serving any food.*

Language Arts: A PEBBLE FOR YOU

Share the following poem with your students:

PEBBLES

Pebbles belong to no one
Until you pick them up —
Then they are yours.

But which, of all the world's
Mountains of little broken stones
Will you choose to keep?

The smooth black, the white,
The rough gray with sparks
Shining in the cracks?

Somewhere the best pebble must
Lie hidden, meant for you
If you can find it.

—*Valerie Worth*

Place a pile of pebbles on a table. Invite each student to choose one of the pebbles to keep. Gather students in a circle on the carpet. Let students take turns describing their rocks and telling why they chose them. Invite students to incorporate the rock into a story during their writing time. Give each child a copy of the poem to share at home. (See page 102.)

Literature Connections

It Could Still Be a Rock
by Allen Fowler (Children's Press, 1991). This book explores the size, shape, composition, origin, and other characteristics of different kinds of rocks.

On My Beach There Are Many Pebbles
by Leo Lionni (Mulberry Books, 1995). Look at the pebbles on a beach—fishpebbles, goosepebbles, numberpebbles, and letterpebbles.

Stone Soup
by Marcia Brown (Atheneum Publications, 1989). This story, based on an old French tale, is about three hungry soldiers who trick greedy villagers into providing them with a feast.

Sylvester and the Magic Pebble
by William Steig (Simon and Schuster, 1989). When Sylvester finds a magic pebble, he wishes himself to be a rock to escape a lion. Now his parents are out looking for him, and he wants to be a donkey again.

Greater Than, Less Than, Equal To

Name _____   Date _____

This is what my rock looks like:

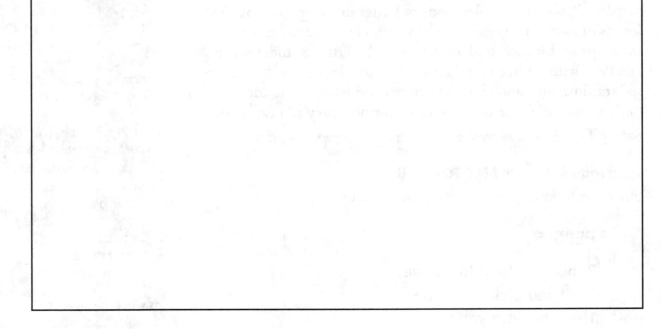

This is how much my rock weighs: _____

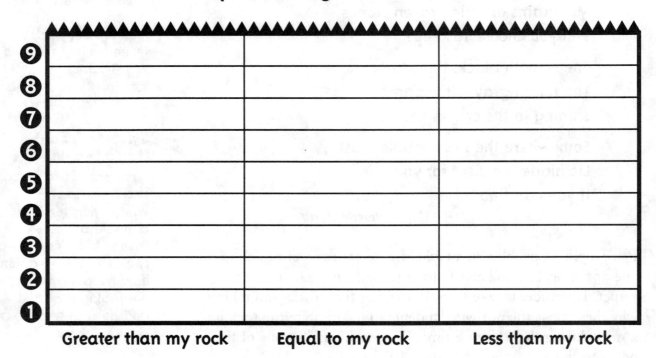

9			
8			
7			
6			
5			
4			
3			
2			
1			

Greater than my rock   Equal to my rock   Less than my rock

Name _____ **Date** _____

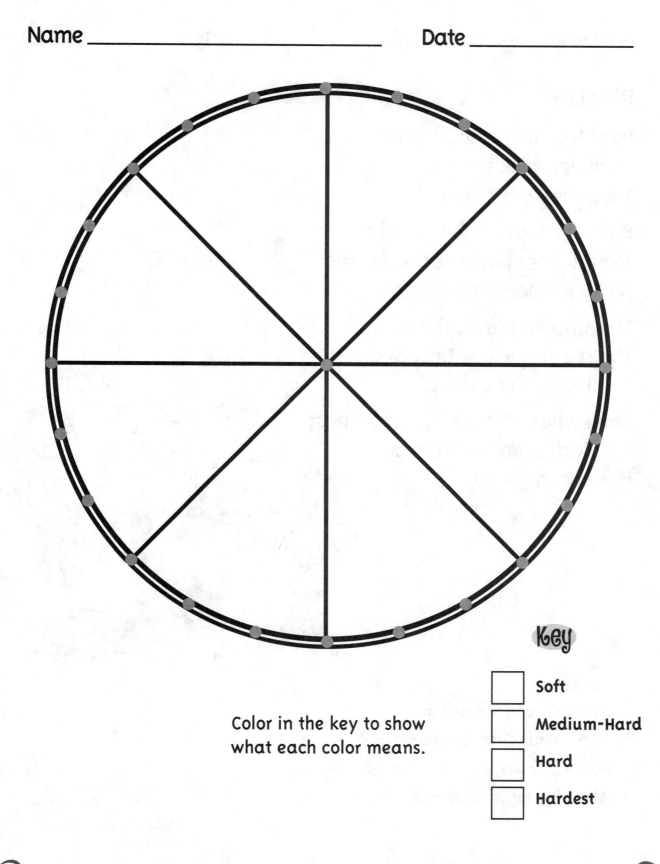

Color in the key to show
what each color means.

Key

☐ Soft

☐ Medium-Hard

☐ Hard

☐ Hardest

Name _____ Date _____

PEBBLES

Pebbles belong to no one
Until you pick them up –
Then they are yours.

But which, of all the world's
Mountains of little broken stones
Will you choose to keep?

The smooth black, the white,
The rough gray with sparks
Shining in the cracks?

Somewhere the best pebble must
Lie hidden, meant for you
If you can find it.

—*Valerie Worth*

Try This!

Start a rock collection at home.

- What words describe your rocks?

- How many ways can you sort your rocks?

- Which is your favorite rock? Why?

"Pebbles" by Valerie Worth. From SMALL POEMS by Valerie Worth. Copyright © 1972 by Valerie Worth. Reprinted by permission of Farrar, Straus & Giroux.

Dig Into Sand

Want your students to dig math? Bring in some sand! Children can sift through a tub of sand to search for coins to count. Add some containers to the setup to measure and compare how much sand each one holds. Sand in soda bottles makes sand timers. That's just the beginning of what happens when you let students dig in to sand!

• **Related Themes: Rocks, Ocean, Beach**

Treasure Hunt

After digging up coins buried in sand, students make rubbings, count the change, and record the total.

Skills and Concepts: counting change

Steps

1 Bury some coins in the tub of sand and place it at a center with some paper.

2 Let students visit the center and search through the sand for the buried treasure.

3 Have students place the coins they find under paper and make rubbings. Ask students to count the coins and write the total value next to their rubbings.

Materials

- coins
- plastic dish tub
- play sand
- paper
- crayons

Sandpaper Counting Books

Students make counting books from rubbings of sandpaper numerals.

Skills and Concepts: numeral writing, numerical order, counting by ones

Steps

1 Cut the numerals 1 to 10 out of sandpaper.

2 Place loops of masking tape on the back of each numeral. Attach the numerals to a flat surface at a work space.

3 Let students visit the center and make rubbings of each numeral by placing paper on top of a numeral and rubbing it with a crayon.

4 Have students cut out their numerals and glue them to construction paper, one per sheet. Have students sequence the pages and draw seashells to correspond with the numeral on each page.

5 Staple students' pages together between construction paper covers. Let them give their books a title and read them to one another.

Materials

- **sandpaper**
- **scissors**
- **masking tape**
- **paper** (ten sheets per child)
- **crayons**
- **construction paper** (ten sheets per child)

Tip

Sand is available at building supply stores. Make sure the sand you use is labeled "Play Sand." Other sand can contain substances that are unsafe for children.

Sand Weights

Challenge students to sequence five containers of sand from heaviest to lightest.

Skills and Concepts: measurement of weight

Steps

1 Fill five margarine tubs with different amounts of sand. Label them 1 to 5. Place them at a center with copies of the Sand Weights record sheet.

2 Let students take turns visiting the center and comparing the different amounts of sand. Have them do this not by looking in the containers, but by holding up two containers at one time (one in the palm of each hand) and feeling which is heavier. Ask students to arrange the containers from heaviest to lightest and record results on their record sheets.

3 After all students have had a chance to visit the center, gather them together in a circle. Request that they bring their record sheets and a pencil. Place a balance scale or a bathroom scale in the middle of the circle.

4 Use the scale to accurately determine the order of the containers from heaviest to lightest. Have students write this information on their record sheets. Guide students in comparing their results by asking these questions:

✿ How different were your results from your guesses?

✿ Was it easy or difficult to compare the containers by lifting two at a time?

✿ Can you think of a time when you might need to know how heavy an object is? Which method would you use to determine its weight?

Materials

- **five margarine tubs with same-size lids**
- **sand**
- **marker**
- **Sand Weights record sheet** (see page 109)
- **paper**
- **pencils**
- **balance scale or bathroom scale**

Sand Timer

Make a sand timer with students and let them estimate the number of seconds it will take for the sand to run down.

Skills and Concepts: measurement of time

Materials

- **two one-liter bottles**
- **cardboard**
- **hole punch**
- **sand**
- **funnel**
- **masking tape**
- **Sand Timer record sheet** (see page 110)
- **stopwatch or clock with a second hand**

Steps

1 Tell students that before people had clocks, there were other tools for keeping track of time. One such tool was an *ampolleta* (am-poe-YET-ah), which is Spanish for *sand timer*. Columbus used these half-hour sand timers to keep time on his ships.

2 Make a sand timer with students. Place a one-liter bottle upside down on top of a sheet of cardboard. Trace around the top of the bottle and cut out the circle. Using a hole punch, make a hole in the center of the cardboard circle.

3 Pour one cup of sand into the bottle using a funnel. Take the cardboard circle and tape it to the top of the bottle. Make sure that the tape is not covering the hole in the center of the circle. Place a second one-liter bottle on top of the first bottle. Tape the two bottles together. Make sure the rims meet.

4 Gather students in a circle. Ask them to estimate how many seconds it will take for the sand to empty from one container to the other. Have them write their estimates on their record sheets.

5 Let the sand timer run and measure its time against a stopwatch or a clock with a second hand. Share the actual time and have students record it on their record sheets.

6 Have students name activities they could do in that amount of time. Ask: *Could you read a whole book? How about a page?* Have students draw a picture of something they could do in that amount of time in the space provided on the record sheet.

7 Add or take away sand from the sand timer and repeat steps 4 to 6.

Which Holds More?

Which container holds the most sand? Students predict, record, and measure to find out.

Skills and Concepts: volume

Steps

1 Label the first four containers (different sizes and shapes) numbers 1 to 4. Gather students in a circle. Place the containers in the center.

2 Ask students which container they think will hold the most sand. Have them record their predictions on the the record sheets under Part 1.

3 Using a one-cup measure, begin scooping sand into container 1. Have students count the cups aloud and record the total on their record sheets. Repeat with containers 2 to 4 and have students record results.

4 Have students look at their record sheets. Ask:

   ✿ Which container holds the most sand?
   ✿ Which holds the least?
   ✿ Were you surprised by the results?

5 Show students the two containers that have the same volume but are different shapes. Repeat steps 2 and 3 (having students record results under Part 2) and discuss results. Ask students why one of the two containers might look as if it would hold more even though it doesn't.

6 Take another container, one not used in the other activities, and ask students to estimate how many cups of sand they think it will hold. Let them share their estimations by holding up that many fingers.

7 Begin scooping sand into the container and counting the cups aloud with the students. Repeat steps 6 and 7 using different-size containers.

❡ Materials ❡

- **four containers** (different sizes and shapes)
- **Which Holds More? record sheet** (see page 111)
- **measuring cup**
- **sand** (enough to fill the largest container)
- **two containers** (same size, different shapes)
- **one to three containers** (any size, any shape)

Literature Connections

From Sand to Glass
by Ali Mitgutsch (Carolrhoda Books, 1983). Learn about glass-making from the melting of sand in a furnace with soda, lime, and recycled glass to the molten glass that is rolled into window panes and blown into bottles and jars.

Sand Cake
by Frank Asch (Gareth Stevens, 1993). Papa Bear concocts a sand cake using his culinary skills and a little imagination.

Sand in My Shoes
by Wendy Kesselman (Hyperion, 1995). A child says good-bye to a summertime of fun at the beach and vows not to lose the shell in her pocket once she returns to the city.

Summer Sands
by Sherry Garland (Gulliver Books, 1995). A beach community works together to restore the dunes after they've been destroyed by a winter storm.

Extra, Extra...

Social Studies: SAND CLAY

For thousands of years, people have used sand (mixed with other natural ingredients) to create bricks, pots, and other items. Mix up some sand clay for students to use.

- Mix one cup play sand with one cup cornstarch and one cup boiling water (teacher only). Stir until the mixture cools.

- Let students create objects with the clay. Bake in a 300° Fahrenheit oven for one hour.

Music and Movement: SAND SHAKERS

Fill small containers with sand. Glue or tape the lids on tightly. Pass them out and invite students to use them as percussion instruments while reading a poem or singing a song.

Game: PAPAGO

Here's a traditional Native American game to play. Divide the class into two teams. Provide each team with four cups of sand and one marble. Have each team hide the marble in one of the cups. Let the other team guess the location. Teams receive points based on the number of guesses. The first team to score 50 points wins the game.

First try = 10 points, **Second try** = 6 points, **Third try** = 4 points, **Fourth try** = 0 points

Science and Nature: FROM ROCKS TO SAND

Give each child a copy of the poem (see page 112) and read it aloud.

ROCKS

Big rocks into pebbles,
pebbles into sand.
I really hold a million million rocks here in my hands.

—*Florence Parry Heide*

Show students how sand forms by pounding a pebble with a hammer. (Put the pebble in a resealable bag first and keep students at a distance while doing this.) Explain that the hammer is like waves washing against a rocky shore.

Name _____ **Date** _____

What is the order of the containers from heavier to lightest? Number them to show your predictions.

My Predictions

Number the containers to show the order from heaviest to lightest.

My Results

heaviest

lightest

Sand Timer

Name _____   Date _____

Sand Timer	**PREDICTION** How long will it take for the sand to empty?	**RESULT** How long it took for the sand to empty.	Something I can do in this amount of time.
1			
2			
3			

Hands-On Math Around the Year • Scholastic Professional Books

Which Holds More?

Name _____   Date _____

Part 1

- **MY PREDICTION**

  Container _____ will hold the most sand.

- **RESULTS**

  Container 1: _____ cups   Container 2: _____ cups

  Container 3: _____ cups   Container 4: _____ cups

Part 2

- **MY PREDICTION**

  Container _____ will hold the most sand.

- **RESULTS**

  Container 1: _____ cups   Container 2: _____ cups

Name _____   Date _____

ROCKS

Big rocks into pebbles,

pebbles into sand.

I really hold a million million rocks here in my hands.

—*Florence Parry Heide*

Try This!

- Circle the word *sand*. Write three words that rhyme with *sand*.

_____   _____   _____

- What other things do you think you can hold a million of in your hand?

_____

_____

_____